THE NEW EARTH

THE SEQUEL TO THE STORY OF LOVE AND CREATION

MAURENE WATSON

Published By

Note for Librarians: A cataloguing record for this book is available from Library and Archives Canada at www.collectionscanada.ca/amicus/index-e.html
ISBN 1-4251-1012-6

Printed in Victoria, BC, Canada. Printed on paper with minimum 30% recycled fibre.
Trafford's print shop runs on "green energy" from solar, wind and other environmentally-friendly power sources.

TRAFFORD
PUBLISHING™
Offices in Canada, USA, Ireland and UK

Book sales for North America and international:
Trafford Publishing, 6E–2333 Government St.,
Victoria, BC V8T 4P4 CANADA
phone 250 383 6864 (toll-free 1 888 232 4444)
fax 250 383 6804; email to orders@trafford.com
Book sales in Europe:
Trafford Publishing (UK) Limited, 9 Park End Street, 2nd Floor
Oxford, UK OX1 1HH UNITED KINGDOM
phone 44 (0)1865 722 113 (local rate 0845 230 9601)
facsimile 44 (0)1865 722 868; info.uk@trafford.com
Order online at:
trafford.com/06-2771

10 9 8 7 6 5 4 3 2

TABLE OF CONTENTS

THE NEW EARTH

PART ONE

In the following chapters, you will read articles that will help you understand the progression of what is required to leave the old Earth behind and to join in: new thought, feelings, and attitudes in every system across the planet. These new thought systems will manifest as: communities, planetary regeneration centers, universities, counsels, and/or inter-dimensional communication centers. They will serve the greatest good for all humanity in order to move back into a natural expression of unified love!

The New Earth could not be built until, enough humans agreed, to resolve enough of their prior Earth conflicts at the: planetary, solar, and universal DNA memory levels, in order to proceed to the next stage in evolution. This was an absolute necessity, because the next stage in evolution requires a perquisite of, unconditional love in the cell of each human being.

The reader is guided to reference the original text, **The Story of Love and Creation: <u>www.trafford.com/robots/03-0615.html</u>** for an in depth understanding of the old Earth phenomena and history matrix.

PART TWO

The second part of the book contains a **<u>Workbook</u>** with sequential **<u>Exercises</u>** that show the application of the restoration, or re-imprint, of the DNA mapping process for the self mastery of: the human, the soul, and spirit merge process to overcome death, disease, and suffering in the human form. Mankind, then will parallel as steward: for the new Earth systems, soul-spirit bodies, quantum sciences, and the re-introduction to the intergalactic community in the applications for mastering our return to living love.

*<u>Note:</u> It is highly recommended that the reader refer to the **<u>definitions and concepts section,</u>** to gain easier and richer comprehension of the articles presented.*

OVERVIEW

IN THE NEW EARTH, THE SEQUEL, TO THE STORY OF LOVE AND CREATION YOU WILL EXPLORE:

Definitions and Concepts: Term

Definitions and Concepts: Terms and definitions needed for merging soul, spirit, and quantum psychology, to splice, recode, and re-imprint your own DNA.

Articles of Information: Exploring a sequential transition, from the old to the New Earth, and why you are here at this time; Questions and Answers.

Workbook Exercises: The individual and group exercises, follow a sequential transition, from the old to the New Earth using the mechanics of the soul to rebirth the soul and rebirth the spirit in the DNA.

Bio References and Sources

Recommendation: Special attention is given to the ordering of ascension symbols by Jayne Chilkes, for recoding the DNA. These 12 symbols directly match the progression of steps in this text to master the soul spirit merge process.

Link: http://theangelschannel.netfirms.com

Story Of Love and Creation
Available now: www.trafford.com/robots/03-0615.html

AUTHOR'S BIOGRAPHY

Maurene has taught quantum psychology and the Sciences of Love in private practice/groups for over 20 years. She has assisted many to awaken to self mastery, and merge; human to soul and soul to spirit, through reading, splicing, and re-imprinting their own DNA; to overcome death in the body. Sessions included: inner child, soul agreements, integrating male/female soul or twin aspects, parallel and future selves and advanced spirit infusion.

Prior to that, she taught special education for 14 yrs. She has a Masters degree in counseling, and a Masters in special education from Boston College. She is a grad of the New England School of Acupuncture, and is proficient in herbal, crystal, cranial, and soul technologies.

Maurene has a profound understanding and dynamic use of the understanding of genetic splicing in the DNA strands and their connection to the neuron-chemistry of the brain. This is the very basis at the root of the new medical sciences coming onto the planet at this time.

She also works with the new DNA understandings with the psychic children. She guides these children as to how best utilize their gifts, while helping their parents to better understand their genius and their role as new leaders and teachers.

Her book outlines the soul spirit merge process along with: DNA holographic imaging, bio- magnetic neural brain cycling/rewiring, inner journeying, and body bio programs, directed by the unique individual/group consciousness of the client's gifts. Readers may reach the author for consults or sessions, at mwatson7@rochester.rr.com or 585-383-0829.

The Melchizedek Ascension Symbols © 2006 ***channeled by Jayne Chilkes***
Available at: *angels3@rochester.rr.com – http://theangelschannel.netfirms.com*
www.trafford.com/robots/03-0615.html

12 Sacred Symbols, 81/2" x11" each, with: Color, Mantra, Sound, and Affirmations channeled by Melchizedek as Ascension Tools for brain balance, twin flame unification, balancing the physical, emotional, mental and spiritual bodies and activating the DNA.

BIOGRAPHY — Jayne Chilkes

Jayne Chilkes has over 25 years experience as an Intuitive Healer, Soul Channel for Twin Flames and the Masters, Hypnotherapist, DNA Practitioner, Musician, Composer and Artist.

She has written two books, *The Call of an Angel* and *Twelve Steps to Heaven*, composed music tapes and CDs, and created the Chakra Cards as well as The Melchizedek Ascension Symbols.

Jayne is available for personal sessions and workshops: angels3@rochester.rr.com

Related Sources

Jayne Chilkes
Link: http://theangelschannel.netfirms.com *-to order Ascension Symbols*

Ramtha Discourses
Link: http://www. Ramtha. com

Taylor, John C. In Gabriel Discourses.
Link: http://home. at. net/~john. Gabrieldiscourses

Watson, Maurene. The Story Of Love And Creation.
Link: www. trafford. com/robots/03-0615. html

EARTH MODEL FOR FAMILIES

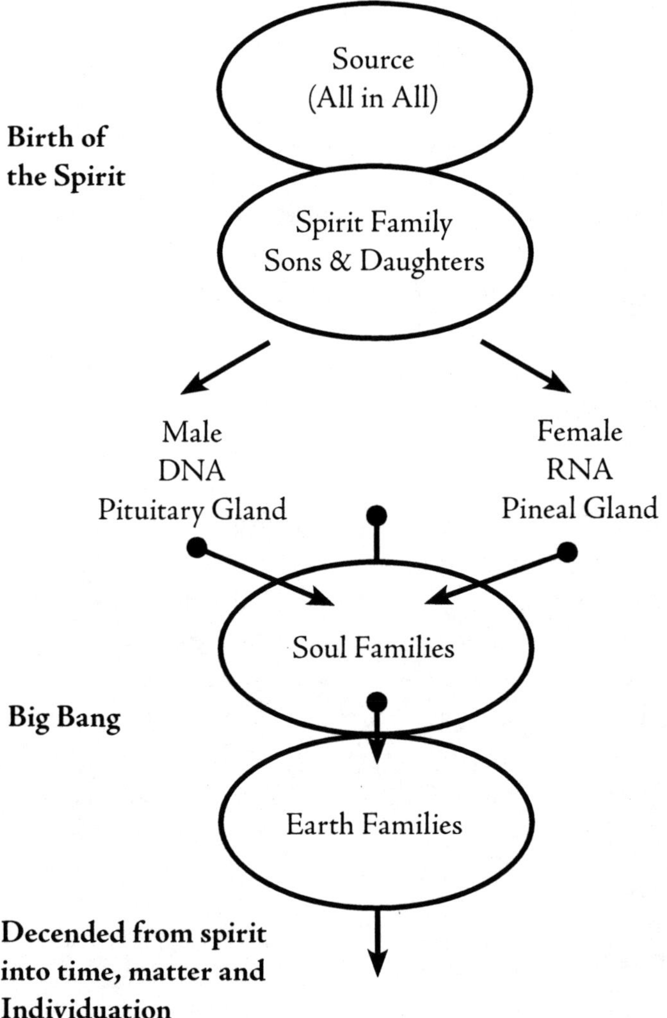

DEFINITIONS AND CONCEPTS

Altered ego – See also ego

When active in negative thoughts, feelings, attitudes, or beliefs, our limited self will engage in predominately fear-based limitations. The limited self will recycle childhood traumas and victimizations that have shattered the self identity, or threatened our sense of self. In the human experience, serious fragmentations of ego identity can act like one has multiple selves or sub personalities. At the soul level, we call these aspects of self, or lifetimes, soul fragments. Imagine all the lifetimes in a body where you had to struggle with the fears of your altered ego.

Those memories are recorded in the memory of the body you are now living in.

The ego designates it whole job as keeping the body alive at all cost. Hence, it alters or becomes altered from its once healthy condition, and goes into fear engaging in the following limited emotional states: fear, anger, blame, shame, hate, resentment, judgment of self/other, justification, projection, bondage, thought distortion, obsessions, competition, confrontations, greed, lust, suffering, pain, destruction, sexual aberrations, addictions, or relationship fears, negative self-expression, self-indulgence or delusions of power. The degree of fear usually dictates adaptability and functioning. Judgment of self or others justifies resistance to change. Healthy, aware, egos promote optimum character development!

Astrology

This is a belief system that the position of the constellations and planets in our solar system, at the exact date and time we are born on Earth, can dictate our reality. This can be a limited belief system unless it is used as a map, a tool, or a guide to our own knowing. There is a fascination with this tool mostly because it seems to strike deeply into the loss of our original Soul-

Spirit memory and our search for "Home", and where we came and went from before Earth.

Its original intent was to provide a map (or template) as to remember where we had been in the universe so we would not forget who we were, where we came from, and the lessons that the Soul-Spirit DNA had yet to accomplish to complete Earth studies. There are many planets, systems, solar bodies, and parallel universes that will be discovered as we become intergalactic and universal citizens again. Certainly, new systems of astrology will evolve!

Balancing Gender

The spirit is androgynous. However, the soul families expressed gender, through the merge of the Creational Mother and Creational Father Matrixes given from Divine design. This has allowed the human, an equal experience of male/female bodies. The soul expresses differ DNA attributestranding or qualities, for male/female emotions, through accessing both the right/left hemispheres of the brain in balance.

Consciousness

This is the level, where one is aware of their thoughts, feelings, attitudes, and beliefs rather than that which the outer world accepts as the only truth. This can be called the "connection to the God within". Here, one's inner awareness of truth comes from their inner experience, which then dictates the outer experience. Self loves, and self awareness, are the main elements. Wherever your focus or attention of energy is, will your consciousness follow!

DNA Information

There are over 120,000 genes in the human genome. The protein-encoded portions of DNA, the buildings blocks of life, are constantly being regenerated within the body. The intelligence of the design and the part that represents your unique instruction sits in the RNA, which is only 3%, and represents the majority of your DNA. The other 97% or, "junk DNA," is shared by the collective or the rest of the people on the planet and in our cosmos. The DNA/RNA is written in an inter-dimensional language which encodes through base-twelve math. This information is the map for the soul spirit's agenda and codes every cell, organ, gland and brain function. It contains a multi-dimensional memory bank of both your personal records of experience as well as the universal records of experience.

Ego

This is a sense of self that sets a boundary between one's inner world and outer world. It is an adaptive defensive physic-psychological mechanism that allows one to stay in a body and digest human experience without being overwhelmed by fear, developing disease, or experiencing death. The ego analyzes data from the mental, emotional, physical, and spiritual bodies. It draws daily conclusions that allow for temperate and safe people, places, circumstances, and events in one's life space. This provides maximum growth in the constant process of re-identification of the self.

The healthy ego operates in knowing that, one has a right to one's own identity, and is enough. Both strengths and weaknesses are allowed within the Self. One can love and be loved in equal balance. One can feel and talk about one's feelings, and is not afraid to be vulnerable. Life is a progressive experience of diversity, change, and problem solving. Imagination, adventure, and an overall sense of play are motivators. This does not mean that one is not challenged to overcome childhood or genetic programming and assume responsibility for change. There is an acceptance, surrender, and realistic detachment that life is a process that develops character, allowing for intimate interactions with others, that are going through similar life experiences and lessons to gain needed wisdom from any limitations.

Grace within Forgiveness and Love

This means that you are forgiven before you started. You were fully sanctioned to create here in free will and free choice bringing all misperceptions and judgments on self or other back to love. Grace says that all actions and emotions are protected by Spirit and all life is sacred. The ultra-violet unconditional love frequency in the brain: dissolves, consumes, forgives, resolves, and baptizes any experience to greater understanding and ownership. The knowing and love of the experience is now kept without the gnawing fear and limitations.

Holy Breath

The breath cycles the changes in the brain. The lower cerebellum at the base of the neck in every human is a life's hard drive and stores the memory of any life form of anything that has ever existed in this universe. This is where the brain releases past DNA programs or can access new ones and communicate this information throughout the body, via the spine.The breath short-circuits the neo-cortex or "monkey-mind" from event memory long enough to allow the new neuron-net brain chemistry to fire the new/next movie image on the screen. This image may or may not be contaminated by the past. So it is the breath that clears the old toxic thoughts, feelings, attitudes, and beliefs, as well as re-imprints the next compelling experience/adventure. The breath ignites and replicates new brain cycles or creative thought, from an image onto the frontal lobe to the midbrain, and to the lower cerebellum, and out through the body, so desires can take form.

Inner Child

The inner child is that part of you who remembers every moment of your life. He/she acts and reacts to situations as an adult based on those experiences. The inner child of this life remembers all other incarnations and existences, stored in the unconscious patterning in the neuron-chemistry of the brain and all the cells of the body. Tapping into the inner child's, triggers the DNA blueprint to stimulate the wounded memory recordings of the soul agenda to change or resolve life's lessons. This in turn stimulates the DNA of the spirit to create new experiences from the life plan.The DNA blueprint is located in the pineal gland. The RNA blueprint is located in the pituitary gland.

Law of Love

Whatever you focus your consciousness on, and put your energy into most, is exactly what you manifest; just like a magnet. Your focused imagination could be considered as you Love and the most important asset in all of creation.

Manifestation

This is the process of creating things visible. The neo-cortex is solution and language oriented, and is also where the collective unconscious mind resides. Linear thinking can be by- passed through resolving polarity, in order to reach the mid or physic brain, which collapses time and opens to higher and higher brain cycle imaging, where the field of potentials can be accessed. The more one is free from the limited thought or social consciousness of persons, places, circumstances, or events, the quicker that the thought can be imaged and imprinted on the frontal lobe in the higher physic brain centers, instead of stuck in the neo-cortex or linear mind brain like a recycled disk, to become a thing.

Mirrors of Love

Love acts as a magnet. Everything in the outer world is set up as a stage with a mirror to reflect back to us that which is held in our thoughts, feelings, attitudes, and beliefs, both of a positive or negative nature. We unconsciously tell others what to do or say to us so that the greatest wisdom can be gained over our thoughts and feelings. If we are holding anger in our electro-magnetic energy field, then our boss will act that out for us. If we refuse to feel, then our spouse may break down and cry. If we are too serious, then our child may nag us to play. So is the stage of life, until we are unconditionally accepting of self and others.

New Spirit Guides, Angels, Cosmic Beings, or Divas

When we have learned certain lessons or finished chosen experiences, we are assigned new guides. Guidance information is processed through frequency patterns in the brain stimulating the DNA. These guides represent a certain focus or expertise that you need at any given time. You can choose from: your soul- a parallel aspect of yourself; from soul families- a pattern of archetypal energies such as the divine mother/father energies; from a master energy such as- the Buddha, Germaine, Christ; from Angelic guides of the plant or crystal kingdoms including- the Elementals of earth, air, fire, water, or metal, or guides from the animal kingdom.

Out of Body Experiences (OBE)

This involves the separation of the body and the consciousness. The ancient Tibetan Book of the Dead describes the steps in the passage of going beyond death through the lower astral vibration levels, or hertzian and infrared frequency bands, to the soul planes. The soul and spirit planes require higher frequencies in the brain: visible, ultra-violet, X-ray, gamma ray, and cosmic light spectrums.The goal of the soul- spirit is to be able manifest at will, to alter matter, energy, space and time, within a totally conscious body.

Soul Agreements

We choose our human family of origin, a well as the body we are in, and all other people, places, and events, to complete the human experience. These lesson plans are the blueprints stored in our DNA. In these bodies, we re-create the past to work out our wounds and turn them into gifts. The soul families exchanged many roles: father, mother, daughter, priest, warrior, and all other archetypes. These families, in the old Earth story, scattered themselves across the universe and lost access to their DNA memories, due to universal traumas including: negative emotional programming, genetic manipulation, and war. This put the pure essence, or organic love DNA, at risk. We are finally healing these programs throughout the mass consciousnessof planet Earth. Tis will in turn, heal the rest of the cosmos, since Earth has DNA representatives from all other creations here. If we judged an experience in one lifetime, or existence, we were compelled to recycle it in another lifetime in order to, allow in love, what we chose to learn about self.

Soul Spirit

The soul spirit operates according to your beliefs. The spirit could be called, "Your pure and uncontaminated origination, DNA love point". The soul is the recorder of your experience. Its pure function was to relay information so that negative experiences do not have to be repeated over and over in order to gain wisdom from them. This could also be called "conscience". The soul is always trying to stay in alignment with the Spirit's agenda to complete the human, or matter, experience, in spite of any limited programs wrought from

DNA memory loss. The Spirit asks only one question, "Do you love me?"

The Spirit knows your past, present, and future. It is your friend, your lover, and provider of all your needs. It is the observer. If there is a particular limited thought that you hold, such as victimization, then the soul will bring into your frequency people, places, times, and events of victimization. Spirit continues to bring in these experiences until completion with the wisdom gained, allows a new choice that is more self-loving.

Spirit Families

The Spirit is composed of parent families that came from the merge of the Father/Mother Matrixes to create this universe. These lifetimes or existences may either be taken in: matter states, light states, or anti-matter void states or existences. They can range from pinpoints of consciousness to formless states, or dense matter. In analogy, it may be easier to think of the soul, as incarnation bodies in male and female forms, and Spirit as expressions of light, color, or sound patterns. It was common practice for spirit beings to embody in the blueprints of the: human, animal, plant, and crystal life forms that they had created. This helped in the practice of lowering the frequency of vibration into mass and matter. The Divine Intent and Purpose from the Creator was already coded within all families.

The Creational Multiple Universe

The ALL In ALL (or Source) focuses through the Mother/Father God families to create individuated self-defining expressions for this universe. The focus of spiritual material mastery incorporates free will, in material universes completing polarity evolution, and moves into an infinite potential of expression; all for the purpose of self love, self reflection and awareness, dynamic experience, and service. All of this is done in the human angel-hybrid cellular body to re-discover love in the cells.

The Creational Mother Matrix

In our universe the mother matrix holds the design for loving and creating from the female principal. She represents the spirit memory of home, hearth, children, bonding to life, and unconditional love in partnership and all relationships. She is the life carrier of new generations through the Divine Mother encoding within her DNA. She is the womb of imagination, or the "inner light". Her marriage partner is the Father Matrix, and together, they spawn new worlds. They are equal in partnership, but different in function.

The Aberrant Mother

She is focused on dark and heavy emotions, which replace sisterhood and bonding. She will abandon, abuse, enmesh, and use her partner or children for her own needs. She will compete with other females for power. She destroys in violence rather than recycle in the natural order. She will go into "attack and defend", as a standard defense. She questions whether or not she can hold her own love. Violence replaces natural cycles such as orgasms and volcanoes, and birth becomes violent. Her war with the male is always over the fact that he took prime role as Creator in the creational merge. She feels the pressure of the male helix -RNA to gain control of all the genetic bloodlines. Destroyer replaces creator.

The Creational Father Matrix

The healthy father principle nurtures, supports, and is in service to the female creations. His nature is: manifestation, time, form, structures, functions, architecture, movement, protection, maintenance, problem solving, boundaries, mind, and the preservation of life. All actions and experiences are sacred and no experience is better than another. Forgiveness is inherent within all movement. His will is that of the Divine Father. His genetics are contingent upon the mother's bloodline. His equality is in perpetual support of the mother creations and her focus on love.

The Aberrant Father

Here, power is expressed without love. The false ego postures pure male will without adaptation and change, even to the point of cutting off or altering the Divine DNA love blueprint. The action of creating becomes more important than loving and sharing. The emotional reactions are expressed in: abuse, rage, anger, violence, control, blame, and avoidance of vulnerability as a defense against the creative power of the female. He will kill her, or her children, unless they fit into his forms or beliefs. He lives outside his emotions and expects the female to carry his expression for him. He has a great fear of the Void and fears that he will cease to be if he doesn't control or force the Mother. He competes in wars with other creator gods for control of the universe. Power and control become addictions.

Truth is Subjective Reality- (non-Judgment)

Everyone is right from his or her point of view and vantage point. You never did anything wrong to another, and they never did anything wrong to you. There are no violations in any reality, as all experience is by agreement.

RNA/DNA without The Death Hormone

Our bodies hold all the programming that humans accepted in civilizations and societies prior to, and on Earth. Toxic stress patterns cause the cell to undergo fission and constant death and/ or disease. As the body deletes these programs of limitation, or the altered ego, the death hormone is deleted in the brain neurochemistry. The cell is then able to go into a fusion state, where when one cells dies, another is born instantly in love. Cell fusion also allows original brain DNA/RNA memory to be naturally restored or activated. Our body can, through regenerative cell memory and altered ego purification, live consciously for as long as one chooses. This occurs as the carbon based cell structure returns to its natural crystalline or diamond structure. It is a cell that is nourished by photons of light, rather than food, and communicates through the DNA/ RNA strands in vibration frequency of unconditional love and unity.

Sacred Geometry

Five platonic solid patterns make up the blueprints of physical matter creation and the genesis of form. This universal science explains the energy patterns that create and unify all life forms in organizational patterns and hold the consciousness of all life for the evolution of the human soul- spirit. These natural patterns of growth and movement originate in one or more 3D geometric shapes: the tetrahedron, hexahedron, octahedron, dodecahedron, and icosahedrons. These symmetrical fractal patterns of creation also make up all the molecules of our DNA, including the map for the periodic table of our elements. These life codes are evident in snowflake or crystal patterns, animal or plant signatures, light patterns, or even spiraling stars or galaxies. Each geometric pattern was formed by mathematical, light frequency cycles, as well as musical constants that explained both natural and creational laws. Thus, we could say that all matter is made of light, color, and sound patterns. Before we lowered into mass and matter bodies we created as patterns of light, color, and sound or sacred geometry. We can also call these vibrations, aspects of ourselves in energy of form bodies.

Time Travel Holograms

We inhabit a multi-dimensional universe, in which several dimensions of different vibration states co-exist. Higher dimensions move faster at and above the speed of light. Lower dimensions move slowly until they occupy matter states. The soul can operate many bodies of experience at the same time which we call, parallel lives. Holograms are simply known or unknown time or spatial reference points that converge. These reference points can meet as: thought forms, or brain images associated with people, places, times, events, or circumstances. That is why there can be so many differing viewpoint of history, for example. Where these viewpoints converge, you have a type of hologram. A holographic experience can be likened to having the same experience that everyone on the planet is having, while you're still having your own unique experience of the same.

Holograms come from interrupted light wave fields that contain all life information as a library. This is like having a movie playing in your head where you meet your friends, your ideas, or something for something you desire to know. A desire, a thought, a feeling, searches for knowing to validate itself as a truth. So, your truth is able to look for itself in past and future selves, or parallel reflections of self, while still in the human body, through the library of personal or collective genetic memory. So what fears you resolve in the now, you automatically resolve in the past, present, and future. What joys or evolution you gain now, also relay or experience in the past, present, and future.

Remote Viewing

Remote viewing is the practice of observing an event outside your present moment of your experience, using mental and emotional imaging, in order to access information. By definition, no interaction is allowed, just observation. However, it can be argued that in the moment you observe something you have changed it.

When remote viewing is used, to look at the inner child and past lives in order to consciously heal old wounds to change the past or future, then it is closer to the definition of soul travel, where the observer is allowed direct participation to make changes desired. Governments often use remote viewing to observe circumstances, events or places of other countries for security purposes. In this scenario, human consciousness operates like scanning technology.

Soul travel

Soul travel allows one to travel, or focus their energy into another frequency of experience, while still fully conscious in the body. This begins by closing the eyes, until one begins to feel a shift of vibration in the form of sounds, colors, and electrical body pulses or humming sensations, in the human heart and brain that accompany the movement between time and space. In this high brain wave state, one experiences their own movie, as both observer and participant, of the experience simultaneously. Other realities, time frames, or information are referenced for growth or change.

Wounds

These are thoughts, feelings, attitudes, beliefs, intentions, commitments, choices, spoken words, or actions that are negative. Wounds repeat and recycle over and over, causing stagnation in any area of one's life. They prevent change, growth, and joy and they can be held in the mind, the emotions, the body, or soul DNA memory. These wound programs of negativity come from early childhood and are carried in generations of aberrant DNA; human, soul, and spirit beliefs, contaminating relationships, money as manifestation, the creative work place, and limit the range of positive emotions, thereby draining the life force energy. Some wounds, we are consciously, aware of while most are stored in the subconscious mind. The rest are deeply buried in the memory of the past because we are too afraid to feel them. All the collective wounds on the planet are called stored in the collective unconscious of the global mind, where our planet is positively or negatively affected by our thoughts and feelings. Perhaps, if everyone on the planet stopped suffering there would no longer be tears of rain.

If we no longer took oil from the Earth's ovaries, then would our synthetic plastics cause cancer in our bodies? Would we have terrorists, if we stopped abusing and victimizing others or ourselves!

Examples: Human wounds:

- I'll never be enough.
- I am afraid I'll never be loved for who I am.
- Women are always victimized.
- Everything I eat always makes me fat.
- I start out the day in a good place, and then I get mad.
- Every time I get in a relationship, he/she, leaves me.
- All my bosses are idiots.
- If I drive into the city, I'll probably have an accident.
- Every time I invest in the stock market, I lose everything.

PART ONE

ARTICLES- QUESTIONS AND ANSWERS

Note: It is highly recommended that the reader refer to the definitions and concepts section, to gain easier and richer comprehension of the articles presented.

How do we activate our dormant soul spirit DNA?

ARTICLE- *Understanding Your Cosmos- Your New Genetic Blend*
Completing your Earth school lessons avails you to become a New Genetic blend. Your new genetic blend is: the completion of the soul blueprint, or the resolution of your past, combined with your dormant spirit blueprint, which is activated when you complete the soul's agenda. Both blueprints are already stored in your DNA/RNA.

The soul's agenda is comprised of the completion of polarity or third and fourth density evolution. This means that physical duality lessons: right/wrong, good/evil, male/female, and any other negative thoughts or feelings that cause death, to a once immortal cell, have been resolved or understood for greater understanding or awakening to the soul.

When the cell is no longer battling for its survival wasting its hormones on the fear of death, then a higher frequency of cell fusion, regeneration or unconditional love, is remembered in the DNA blueprint; or the spirit's genetic body. The spirit DNA/RNA is the totality of all life that has ever existed in a pure state of potential. Experiences of the free will choice of learning to give and receive love equally, provide the playground of experience.

On a very practical level, one is able to read, channel, or feel/imagine (DNA) and interpret (RNA) their god cell coding. This is later experienced as a state of feeling/being at One with all life and the understanding that all beings choose realities to create in order to share their self love. (Unity consciousness)

Each cell in the body contains 10 trillion memory units of information. This allows one to tap into their genius, including any talent, gift and ability gained in other lives, which allows one to bring those gifts into the now. We usually draw in, a mirror of a person, place, circumstance, or event to mirror in our daily lives, as an aspect of self that we are trying to master. If we contain self hatred, then we will magnetically draw an angry partner or situation.

If we believe we are a failure, then our company might well go bankrupt. Whatever you think and feel flows directly through you. The love or fear you feel is attracted back to you and is also sent out to the planet's collective field of experience. In short, the soul creates directly from our beliefs and attitudes.

If you believe the earth will experience devastation, then indeed, your fear is helping to create that for self and al others.

The soul spirit's agenda is to integrate all parallel and future selves. Hence, you can blend your experience learned in your soul blueprint; all past experience, with your original pure spirit blueprint to create a unique blend that you can share, in service to to your own love and humanity. If you have a wounded aspect of self stuck in a time line of war in the French Revolution or the intergalactic wars, then you may well feel that feeling in your daily now, till you resolve the need to war against self or another. The quality, duration, and accumulation of negative emotion dictate, by the laws of attraction, if another lifetime may be needed to resolve that feeling. Once the soul's agenda is complete, your new creations and learning are endless, because one has the opportunity to combine the learning of the past with a blend of future self potentials for the spirit's agenda. This new blend is one of god-man self realized, self aware, and self loving in a human body having mastered matter, time, and form.

Earth has representatives from all universes, with differing genetic blends, which have come to heal their past wounds and bring in a more evolved future. The rebirth of each human soul serves in tandem with the birth of the new Earth in bringing in a new and unprecedented blend of a universal DNA.

This genetic blend is comprised of many different genetic races that were originally birthed into this universe ten billion years ago. They agreed to study polarity in matter evolution, along with free will, in order to study creation in both matter and spirit. In this way all creations before and after this one could be blended into a new future.

Changing the future templates with your imagination replicates the DNA while using unconditional love in the cells to collapse time, with this love being self awareness or consciousness in the cells When we tap into the mid or physic brain centers using the frontal lobe as an imaging device, by holding an image on our movie screen or pineal gland for a minimum of 17 seconds, we activate that creation to the speed of love/light or beyond. The manifestation will return if there are no negative thought/feeling patterns stuck in the limited neo cortex brain in the way, to receive your desired imagine.

Whatever we ask in our own behalf is sent out to the planet in a measure of the frequency we carry. This is what Grace offers as a witness of love. The brain frequencies are: hertz, infrared, visible light, ultraviolet, X-ray, gamma ray, and cosmic ray. The midbrain stimulates direct access through the DNA/RNA abilities of: clairvoyance, clairaudience, telepathy, bi-location, clairsentience, and super consciousness latent within the brain. When you collapse time by moving into a feeling of unconditional love, you are using the scientific formula to time travel by bending light and folding time, and even the ability to move your consciousness through wormholes to other universes. Can the human body be the model for this? How can we activate our own genetic blends in our own body?

Nothing is missing when you are connected to the self. How does one know what to do, where to go, or who to share with in any given moment? Knowing comes from the intuitive body through the pure thought of love. Thoughts can only become real things or experiences when they are felt. Ow can you feel through thinking. One can easily track the circle of life through all the negative and positive emotions and come back to love. Here the heart is ever neutral and ready to choose needs, wants, desires, passions and imaging, to create a new experience! When you sit inside your own body, inside your own Holy Presence quietly, collapsing time, and imprinting a virgin thought image on your pineal and pituitary gland, you are Love.

The data base from the lower cerebellum is the hard drive of the universal memory. The cerebellum signals the arc of the pineal and pituitary glands, firing up the neuron transmitters and regenerating off the DNA/RNA blueprints. This sends the request for life throughout the spine into the electro-magnetic field around the body, where it is sent into the quantum field of potentials to be returned like magic.

What magic can you send for, from your multiple futures? Your soul spirit will select the energy pattern that you most need to evolve, change, and grow in your very own moment! What lessons have you left to complete? What gifts have you yet to share?

The character attributes in the DNA sequencing are based on mastered experience through an emotional base. This is the main channel to the soul spirit. Negative blueprints of learning from the past contain: suffering, hate, judgment and other polarity emotions or thoughts. One completed, the natural blueprints that fire from thought forms of unconditional love contain: independence, detachment, compassion, resourcefulness, determination, and on. What's in your DNA? The human angel, which is the prize of all universes in its ability to feel, image, choose, and create in an Eternal body.

Where did the earth model for families come from?

ARTICLE *- UNDERSTANDING OUR ORIGINS FROM THE MOTHER/FATHER CREATIONS- The Divine Parenting Roles That Spawned the Collective Unconscious of Earth:*
At the base of understanding all relationships and all human dynamics of family issues remains an explanation of the dramatic argument between the Our Spiritual Parents, or the mother/father within, who have become our human parents. As you read this, you will feel your very soul heal in its own understanding of the need to blend male and female emotion.

Your connection to the Mother God mirrors your own inner connection to your female: the woman you are now, and have been in other lives as well as, all the mothers, wives, sisters, girl children, female lovers, you have been. You could also add the archetypal roles, such as: priestess, leader,_scholar, and so on.

Your connection to the Father God mirrors your own inner connection your male: the man you are now, and have been in other lives as well as: all the husbands, fathers, brothers, boy children, male lovers, you have been. You could also add the archetypal roles, such as: priest, king, warrior, and so on. So, you see the importance of the mother-father connection as the mirror for the base of all relationships on this planet.

The Creational Mother Matrix

The Healthy Mother is the first principle of love and bonding. She is the right to exist. She does not kill unless in an aberrant state. She does, however, recycle life as needed. This is often mislabeled as a destroyer aspect, which is out of harmony with Divine Law. She cycles all emotions through earth, air, fire, water, and ether. She represents home, hearth, children, heart, bonding to live, unconditional love, relationship, and partnership. She must express her feelings, her creativity and will feel a vast range of positive and negative emotions and come back to love, knowing that her love protects all emotions.

She makes all experiences safe, protecting the right to life and free will. She is the heart of the imagination and her desires are raw, primordial, and instinctual. Her will is natural law. The void is her womb space and the birthplace of her creativity and the focus of her love.

The Aberrant Mother is focused on dark and heavy emotions, which replace sisterhood and bonding. She will abandon, abuse, and use her children for her own needs. She will compete with other females for power. She even becomes the dark primordial abyss that devours males and can shape shift into any of the twelve archetypes: warrior, dark priestess, Madonna, Medusa, etc. She is subject to the negative altered-ego as the collective unconscious where pain, shame, blame, judgment and suffering predominate. She destroys in violence rather than recycle in the natural order.

Violence replaces natural cycles as orgasms, volcanoes, and birth become violent. Sexual fantasy replaces imagination and the Divine and ecstatic bliss bodies. Enmeshment: physical, sexual, mental, emotional replace bonding. She feels not enough as a woman and will hide in the Void, sometimes withdrawing the life force and going into involution or further into Black Hole.

She will go into attack and defend as a standard defense. Here she questions whether or not she can hold her own love. She feels banished, parched, and forced into the underworld in sacrifice. Her war with the male is always over the fact that he took prime role as Creator and in the creational merge. She struggles to understand the very male emotion she has agreed to carry in the Divine DNA belly of her creations. Sacrifice has replaced sacred living; fear has replaced imagination and Divine desire. Worst of all, she feels the pressure of the male helix RNA to gain control of all the genetic bloodlines, which by law is her natural function. She experiences male anger, rage, and violence for the first time and feels abandoned, betrayed, and unsupported by the other half of her Soul-Spirit. She had accepted the male genetics in order to sustain a body. In reality, her inexperience, judgment, and fear created a foreign ruler although Cosmic Law says that all experience is by agreement and that there is no violation in any reality.

The Creational Father Matrix

The Healthy Father principle nurtures, supports, and is in service to the female creations through creation and holding of the outer light. His nature is manifestation, time, form building, architecture, movement, protection, maintenance, problem solving, boundaries, mind, and the preservation of life. All actions and experiences are sacred; no experience is better than another. Forgiveness is inherent within all movement. His domain is the external reality and its forms, structures, and functions. His will is that of the Divine Father. His genetics are contingent upon the mother's bloodline. His equality is in perpetual support of the mother creations and her love focus.

The Aberrant Father emotions are locked in the negative archetypes such as the priest, warrior, husband, magician, etc. The emotional reactions are expressed in abuse, rage, anger, violence, control, blame, shame, etc. as a defense against the creative power of the female. He will kill her or her children unless they fit into his forms or ideas. He lives outside his emotions and expects the female to carry their expression for him. He greatly fears the Void and that he will be castrated in the Great Abyss and cease to be. He competes and wars with other creator gods for control of the universe. He is subject to the negative altered-ego and collective unconscious beliefs.

Power without love, postures a false ego. This in turn, postures pure male will without adaptation and change, even to the point of cutting off or altering the Divine DNA blueprint. Here, creating becomes more important than loving and sharing. He will force the mother, the other half of himself, to in volute into Black Hole and lose evolution or hide in the Void if absolute control is needed. Here anger, rage, violence, and fear predominate as male emotions, rather than allowing any vulnerability or wound. These emotions then become confused as a true focus of love. He must keep the mother as second principle of creation to remain in control. This could be called reverse polarization. Power replaces a divine love focus and love is conditional. Love is often a synthetic experience of technology as an avoidance of the experience of true direct emotions. The true father matrix has accepted female genetics in order to sustain a form with heart. His inexperience, judgment, and fear have propelled him into a forced state of addictive power. This is an agreed choice by Soul-Spirit with the mother matrix as well. In free will since there is no violation in any reality

Why are we here on Earth at this time?

ARTICLE- *How Soul Agreements Developed Into Physical Experiences through the Old Earth Stories: (see also-The Story of Love and Creation for an in depth reading of the history of this universe & the story of creation)*
We now explore how the holograms of mother/father creational family patterns affect this life. In coming to Earth at this time, we picked DNA families that would mirror all those emotions and actions, not of love, while keeping the goodness, growth, and joy of life learning. We are forced to remember past negative or reactive emotions such as: judgment, abuse, or fears with self or others, as we face our daily lives. We also can remember through joy!

Everyone in our lives plays a role and acts out what we tell them to do so we can learn from the mirrors of each other. These are the mirrors of love. Once this wisdom of the experience brings understanding and self-awareness, this body is able to cleanse out the toxic pattern through: tears, disease, depression, massage, or any other healing means. The information from this cellular deletion of the negative programs, are immediately sent to all parallel selves in all other simultaneous experiences and any associations with people, places, circumstances and events in those lives.

This is done so that the human and soul family DNA comes into resolution.

The clearance is much like a disease, such as cancer in the DNA line. So too is emotional, mental, and spiritual programming passed from one generation to another. It only takes three generations to alter gene structure of heavy DNA programming. At the end of each program deletion, the body cells must cry or find a way to release the old expressions and toxins, to bring freedom into the physical system. Often this release has been called an ego death.

The body cells can manifest a seeming disease, addiction, depression, or even a state of bliss as the old cell memory leaves. These recorded imprints must be re-experienced in love to rewire the original pure Soul-Spirit DNA in the brain.

The child in this body has to face the pattern of wounds from every aspect of other lives.

Since souls split **into male/female gender bodies**, both male emotional differences as well as female emotional differences must be resolved through some kind of marriage or relationship. In a family Earth marriage, the father usually mirrors the wounded male in the child. The mother usually mirrors the wounded female in a child, regardless of the child's sex. However, you do have souls with more experience in one gender than another serving to balance gender issues and male/female emotions for the human and soul family. A soul usually chooses a gender body where the greatest lessons and growth can occur. At root, is the first relationship the soul had in response to their relationship with the Divine Mother and Divine Father parents' marriage, then the soul parents, human parents, and the parent within? Gender lessons can range anywhere from self-replication memory, issues of physical bonding in cell memory, victimization; or even female souls crossing into male bodies and male souls crossing over into female bodies. Lessons are particular to the pattern of each soul's choice within free will. Speculation can be made that cell bonding in polarity is more resilient than self-replication and promoting immortality and a more resilient DNA body in a mother-father universe.

Our life force body energy that spirals through the DNA and our spine was once used to help create worlds and keep us immortal, before death, fear, and sexual reproduction became aberrations in the DNA codes. Many universes, solar systems, and precious creations were destroyed, returned to the void, or went into black hole.

In the old Earth story, the heart of the Divine Mother felt so overpowered by what she felt as male: force rape, or abuse, as to jeopardize the bonding agent of love of the mother cell principle. Without this as the first signal of love in the child's body, children didn't feel safe and did not feel they had the right to exist. As the male principle could not feel the direct signal of love from the mother, he could not father their creations without force, competition, or connection to her true heart feelings. He felt jealous, rejected, and abandoned, since the mother seemed to be able to withhold her love or keep his baby creations from him. He felt like she had too much power. Does this sound like what we call a divorce on Earth today?

His true nature was to be in equal service to the female. Generations of children became more and more wounded as the human parents misunderstood their natural Divine DNA roles. That is why many races here have repeated the same lessons over and over.

Without the_healthy father-male signals and information to make the physical world reality safe and protected, he too, felt disconnected from heart feelings and concentrated on addictions in the outer world of work, money, time, materiality, competition, movement, and mind. Mother was left to care for all feelings, and the raw creativity behind love. These role boxes were often empty of love. After all, if you put the mother into sacrifice and suffering, there may not be enough love to hold the universe together, as referenced in the aberrant mother/father matrixes. Does this sound like our human divorce?

Many delicate souls, who remained neutral, could no longer function in wounded controlling family matrixes marriages. Often these were more heart-centered, childlike, or creative souls holding to the memory of love where one could create with just a thought. So, they held to their Divine codings, studying in the cosmos and evolving until they could assist their beloved Earth. These beings remembered that the Holy Spirit and the Mother/Father God lived within them as the Presence of All Life lives in The ALL in ALL. They remained less clouded in programming and able to bring great gifts from the past in the form of art, music, new inventive technologies, and societal information and financial systems for the greater good of humanity, throughout various epochs on Earth. They continue to make their way back and forth to Earth with their soul families, to finish their evolution and assist Earth in her soul-spirit merge.

The Mother/Father, creational matrixes, who remained in the distorted concept model, experienced male and female emotion in extreme separation, through judgment.

As we backtrack to the Creational families, we realize that as the distorted monads merged, further creation occurred. Many families fragmented into other solar systems and lost contact with each other. Some families ended up in the wrong creations, read the wrong blueprints and created further DNA genetic distortions with creations that were not from this universe; mixing animal, human, crystal, and plant matrix creations into distortional blueprints. Other creations refused to spawn more families due to their arguments: light is better than dark; male-female twin souls-spirits abusing one another and divoring, genetic seeding manipulations, or the fear of descending into matter.

All this split time into past, present, and future. So whatever happened to the creation families happened to the soul families and was passed into the human families to heal. That is why Earth became the resolution planet for all creations, since other universes now had their genetics here, thinking that they were part of the original experiment. The other simultaneous bodies that each soul spirit family had, recycled more and more experience in density until re-incarnation and the life/death cycle became an addiction. They were hoping eventually, to re-unite and again share their love, as well as try to gather their fragmented selves back together again. In their illusions of perceived separation, fragmented souls began to register seeming fear, loss, or destruction of the physical form they had chosen. The need to resurrect the soul or try to keep it in the body container, without death, began to become a necessity. It is only now that we can even begin to think about retaining the spirit in the human body through the brain DNA blueprints. Many fairy tales and myths are the stories of these higher vibration or inner plane incarnations in a symbolic language.

This colonization and the seeding of the love DNA from Sirius, Andromeda, Arcturus, Pleiades, and various systems and colonized Earth in an attempt to resolve their genetic difficulties or re-seed the divine intent of Earth's Elders. Earth was a playground with all its wonderful gold, minerals, water, primal genetic seeds, and real estate. Species began to barter Earth's genetics and minerals to further, either their agendas of control, or their attempts to return to what they remembered as Source or Home. As more and more came and went from Earth, they brought with them all the polarity memories from the past in their chosen bodies. Each successive body birthed or created, carried continued universal memory particular to each soul and spirit. However, the more trauma and wound perceived, the less the Love DNA memory was retained. The soul body's memory system was still filled with: wars over creating, genetic miscoding, distorted information systems, and divorce in soul and spirit family marriages.

The Earth Adam Kadman, or **human angel body**, was originally coded, to be able to remember the connection to Soul-Spirit in spite of the past. Home would no longer be "out there" but rather, "here". Whatever was remembered or resolved here, even if there were other experiences in other systems, planets, or stars, could be found in the data bank of the embodied vehicle. However, the focus was on the singularity of experience so that many choices could be exercised. Present time had to be the anchor of experience. Earth school became very popular because of the diversity offered in intense and quick evolution and the conquering of self in physical, material mastery using body, mind, and spirit. The nine electrons of creation, coined by Archangel Gabriel: thoughts, feelings, attitudes, beliefs, intentions, commitments, choices, spoken words, and actions, would certainly require a very physical application.

The resolution was to re-print love in the cells, no matter the inflection of the negative or positive feeling, especially judgment, of the chosen experience. This knowing of self, as once being a God and yet, still be able to focus that in the present body experience, would become the coveted challenge. This was to be a living example of a godman in a human body, in a living loving expression of Creator. Creator angel man would descend from the mighty cosmic sun as a creator. He would be a spiritual parent and help genetically code and create a: time, matter, polarized, free will, mother-father universe. He would create all the life forms in it. He could share consciousness with his life forms, but his love would advise him not to: abuse, steal, or destroy his creations. He would descend into the lowest of dimensions learning all he could in/about the physical worlds and return home sharing all that he had learned with his Source, in that his Source would become more.

The experiment allowed evolution in a polarized free will expression; a sanctioned separation. But this turned into extreme free will resulting in: death, suffering, pain, fear, judgments, greed, and lust, forgetting that:

compassion, harmony, peace, divine union, forgiveness, abundance, and unconditional love were already coded in the DNA, as well!

Change has come as an increasing number of experienced souls have been born into each epoch to bring through gifts from many past lives in order to upgrade evolution and keep the polarity moving forward. Higher loving energies will continue as babies are born without polarity and later fully conscious of their God-self memories and experiences, bringing new teachings, gifts, and skills for the next stage of Earth evolution. For, the new children, will want to study and share their gifts in the resolution of this new multiple DNA universe. In simple terms, this is love coming to re-creation-al play of knowing itself from the infinite unknown to matter and back. Perhaps it will be the model for all creators who desire to create their own physical universe one day!

So, love gets re-created through the experience of its creations, in their own biological self-understanding, through the ability to access their own DNA information directly from their Source without mediation. In essence, this is the return of the Holy Spirit in the human biology or any embodiment process. Remember, there are other systems where the human form is not the standard creation. Never again, will an individual lose their unique expression, even in the context of group human family or soul-spirit family, or have to drop their body in enslavement, just to create in any dimension or explore in evolution.

The multi nature of time returns as: co-creational, simultaneous, and holographic. Therefore, the conscious memory progression for clearance beyond death to the next stage of evolution into the twenty first century includes: genetic lifetime patterns, parental relational patterns, and holographic soul patterns. Thus, our new biological-genetic-entity can, through memory, emerge en mass in great pockets of awakening.

Why did I choose my human family?

ARTICLE- *Soul Family Agreements and Integration*
The positive and negative patterns that we bring to our physical bodies and human families of origin come from our Soul families. We normally exchange lifetime roles with them. Sometimes they incarnate as our mothers, fathers, children, or vice versa so that we might learn all the chosen experiences or lessons for the whole group

The Womb

Before we decide to incarnate onto this planet, we hover over our chosen human mother up to one year. When we enter the womb we are prepared to accept our agreements in the DNA and RNA blueprints. We accept that we can complete our lessons or chosen experiences though these parents. This is how the ancestral experiences are passed from one generation to another. Nothing is missing when we are connected to the self. How does one know what to do, where to go, or who to share with in any given moment? Knowing comes from the intuitive body through feeling. Thoughts can only become real things or experiences when they are felt. One cannot feel through thinking. One can easily track the circle of life through all the negative and positive emotions and come back to love. Here the heart is ever neutral and ready to choose: needs, wants, desires, passions and imagination, to create a new experience!

Inner Child memories

Healthy ego development presents at critical growth stages.

It is not till puberty that a child's body begins to process the death hormone from the parental generations. The death hormone, or cellular death, is the secretion in the brain and glandular system of addictive toxic fears and wounded negative thoughts, feelings, or beliefs from the parental DNA that the child must either accept or heal. The child will often carry these for the parents in order to help the parent or gain their acceptance in exchange for love. The process of inner child healing uses guided imagery, color, and sound. Simply, by closing your eyes and focusing on a memory, the potential for healing takes place. We all hold many snapshots of negative experiences. Children develop adaptive defensive mechanisms of the ego system, to protect themselves from further hurt. This happens because they cannot defend themselves once wronged by the parent. The child then shuts down the emotions, leading to depression, anger, stubbornness, competitiveness, rebellion, and a cycle of negative addictive responses. Opening to inner child memories offers an opportunity to resolve those issues that limit and enslave you, in your current life and relationships and prevent the knowing, that it is safe to be loved in a body.

Emotional Dominion

When a child is allowed to trust the healthy progression of their needs, wants, desires, and joys in the full circle of the emotional body, then the imagination is based on self worth, self love, and inner directed passion for growth and adventure. The internal biological guidance system is not reactive and quite naturally flourishes through finding solutions rather than using wounding to learn. **Imagination is an act of mirroring self in embodied love.** Each time you imagine, you replicate your own God DNA.

Why are there so many wounded and suffering humans?

ARTICLE- *Recycling the Abused Child's DNA in Soul and Body to Trust Love* As more and more loves pours from Source to bring forth a rebirth of the human soul and spirit, Mother Earth's wounded and abused children represent the healing for the entire universe. So many of us agonize as to why so many of the Earth children act out this abuse trauma upon this plane.

At the soul level, there is no violation at any level. Every experience is by agreement till the soul completes its learning in the human experience. The abused child endures the experience of stolen love and power passed in the lineage DNA. Most certainly the child is pressed to individuate its own love in the context of a family or group without loosing itself. Why would a parent or Creator god create and have to steal, or even lose the love, from it very own creation, with women and children paying the greatest price? Look around your planet and you will still see the abuse of your own love: in war, greed, torture, abuse to your relationship with the planet and each other, as well as control over the lineages of DNA. We as children must take this torture and planetary fear out of ourselves and return to our natural state of joy and love to assist the birth of the new earth.

What is often not realized by the abused child is that the body will hold these programs as a way to awaken the family of origin or release the ancestors. What happens when the whole identity of a child is based on the agreement for abuse? If the child breaks the negative family pattern, the child feels it will be abandoned or abused even more. What addiction or abuse did your family use? Was it intoxication by money, rage, molestation, denial of feelings, competition, acceptance, threat of abandonment, or violence? The addiction forces you to surrender your free will and natural joy to the parental voices. If the child becomes worthy or joyful then the family secret of abuse gets exposed and the family suffers.

Sacrificing our next generations to Identity Theft of Self

In identity theft addictive behaviors: bulimic, anorexia, drug and sexual abuse patterns all link. This pattern complex could well be called identity theft. The child will give up their identity to one or both parents in order to be loved at the expense of their emotional connection to themselves. The child enmeshes with one or both parents (human, soul, or spirit) in utter dependency to the parent's needs. The need to be perfect to please the parent becomes an addictive bio-chemical response in the brain and body. The ego-self can fragment to such an extreme that the child feels they have no self or appear to have altered personalities. At the highest levels, the bio body will split off from the soul body and the soul body split off from the spirit body.

Love becomes: accommodation, assimilation, fear of death, or enslavement to another's thoughts, feelings, and identity. The child does this to protect itself from abandonment, rejection, and death. The pleasure principle of natural joy and its direct connection to the life force energy (sexual energy) in the body are ruptured. Independent creativity or selfhood is a threat to the parents, in the eyes of the child. The child learns to hide their most intimate feelings and bodily needs. This is dangerous when we consider that the emotional body is a finely tuned instrument, which directly turns on the Holy Spirit DNA connection, which is the most profound and intimate relationship possible. The most precious instrument of love is one's inner thoughts and feelings and connection to the Imagination. When you kill the imagination, you sever the child's connection to their creativity and their Holy Presence and pass on a contaminated DNA.

The addictive substance of love: food, alcohol, drugs, sexual acting out, or abuse; all produce a false endomorphic high in the brain, trying desperately. To breast feed the cells love. One could even call alcoholism the "baby bottle syndrome."

Symptoms include: fear of intimacy, loss of boundaries, numbed, denied, or distorted biological responses, sexual violation or the stealing of power, loss of choices, buried aggression and rage, self hatred, victimization and loss of power, and lacking self trust and self worth. There is no sense of self or connection to one's own soul spirit. True wants, needs, desires, and dreams are abdicated over to another.

Body Imaging: The child displaces a false sense of power and control onto their own body, as they feel; the body is the only thing they can control. Food becomes the only way that they can receive love. Food, abuse or substances replace latent "breast feeding needs," or lost bonding to the mother. The obsession becomes like "a morphine bottle drip", looking for: lost needs, wants, desires or feelings that the mothering/fathering agents of love were unable to provide so the child can bond with their own bodily responses and emotions. The child learns never to be honest and true with him self and to never be comfortable in his/her own skin. Honesty, self respect, self love, self worth is "risky business."

Food or the lack of it has the following associations eating or not eating the abuser's power, or giving them sexual pleasure. These associative feelings becomes the battle ground for "throwing up" self hatred, rage, and control of the parents or significant other in a relationship. It is also a way to expel the parents' physical and psychic energies out of the body so the child can momentarily end the emotional conflicts that leads to self punishment to the body for not being good enough and for not being perfect enough to be loved.

Trusting: Bodily disassociations and responses associated with what we call the life force energy: grooming, sucking, stealing orgasm, penetrating, and often torture behaviors of control, domination, abuse or primal oral behaviors, are passed on from one generation to the next. The molester professes being godlike, while telling the child their very body isn't feeling any of the violence. This causes extreme fragmentation to the emotions, the mind, and body of the child. Often the child is passed around among family members and taught to give such "pleasure" to a sibling. When the contact is not direct, then psychic sexual seduction is often described through the seducer's stalking behaviors or entering the child's dreams.

Sexual energy: This is the life force energy, the raw creative energy, and the direct connection to the soul and the spirit indwelled in the body. Violation to a child's innocence ruptures the imagination which holds the blueprints for life in the brain and glands. When mistrust becomes a neuron-chemical addictive response, then the cells will code to destroy targeted cells through negative emotions.

Soul Level agreements: Many female soul men and male soul women accept such agreements to balance out soul gender issues in their wounded male and wounded male programming for the family of origin, as well as their soul group. Often the sexual translation of the soul's wound or expression can be very confusing, due to the memories stored in the brain's data DNA bank. The program shows at the inner child level, in soul bodies, or even in spirit family memories.

What addiction or abuse did your family use? Was it intoxication by money, rage, molestation, denial of feelings, competition, acceptance, threat of abandonment, or violence?

Healing Applications:

The Abused Child Needs to Speak the Language of Love In Any Healthy Relationship. Affirm Your Own Inner Dialogue with Your Inner Child as You Say These To Yourself:

- We can be together without losing ourselves in each other. I do this by being open, honest, and true with my own needs first.
- We can be together without abandoning each other or hiding our needs.
- We can both have fair boundaries at the same time. I do not lose my identity in you.
- If I am worthy of love, my DNA family will not suffer. My identity was based upon being unworthy or abused so the family secret could be hidden. I carried all the family's secret dark negative feelings of: shame, blame, judgment, hurt, denial, rage, anger, self-hatred, self-destructiveness, violation & mistrust. These were once intoxicating chemical addictions in my body! Self-love flushes these toxins away!
- I give up these negative feelings that once protected me from abuse.
- I now move into my natural state of joy, happiness, unconditional receiving, openness, trust, true self, true choices, and naturalness.

- When I'm unsure, I close my eyes & ask my Spirit to live through me.
- I choose to be with someone who is open, honest, true, and loves who they are.
- I choose to be with someone who doesn't violate them or me?
- I choose to love without manipulation, control, or denial.
- I will learn to love everything about myself, to trust self, and observe self without control.
- I will use the imagination of my inner child to free myself and connect to my Spirit.
- An equal or intimate partner is first a compassionate friend who engages my healthy inner child to play and share joy! I have known my own hurts/needs; therefore I do not batter/abuse another when they share theirs honestly with me.
- I choose not to molest myself with my own anger, suffering, or hurt that others have imposed on me in the past!
- I can choose to work with a body specialist or emotional/mental healer, who can help me delete body programs and restore trust my bio responses.

Further Healing Applications for Abuse:

Changing the Internal Voices of Abuse: The abusive programmed voices in a child's head can alter the cells in the body to receive information that does not support the child's biological health.

The wounded **inner child voice** of an abused person says: "I will test you to see if I can abuse you. If I can abuse you, then I will lose control and act out the same way my mother and father abused me." So strong is the addiction until the body, brain, or emotions kick it out.

The **healthy voice** says: "How do I change the voices that programmed me to accept abuse? How do I get open, honest, and true with my own true feelings in my body saying, no to abuse, and begin to be self aware, self loving, and above all trust self myself again?"

In listening to the **voice of the critical parent**, versus your own voice, there comes a realization, that the adult's voice threw the child out of a direct biological connection to their own bodily responses in order to gain control. The child could not interpret what was going on around him/her except through denial, frozen feelings, rebellion, or shutting down the body or emotions. In the moment of abuse, they must question whose experience· are having and in desperation, try to get back to a small child's reality in a small body. Does the child have to leave the body, hide parent's feeling in the body, or rebel to be free again?

The scars on a child's trust can be overwhelming as they go through life. How do they trust their responses and stay in their own experience? Can they simply ask to be loved? What do they do with these old memories as they come up or recycle? Can they choose to love things away from them, or to them? The secrecy and isolation can keep them deeply hidden in unworthiness!

Methods for Coping with trusting Biological Responses:

- Learn to separate your voice from another's in your head and heart.
- Lovingly, kick your mother/father's voice and emotions, out of your body.
- It is not a child's job to carry this ancestral pain. Delete the wounded male and female voices of your parents from your DNA.
- Once you heal your past, you will see that everything you have been through was to develop character and open you up to an inner soul-spirit guidance system for a higher purpose.
- Remember that each generation is designed to become more evolved than the one before.

Healing Applications: for the Inner language of Abuse:
How do I speak to myself/another in the language of love and unconditional respect as an adult? My inner voice says: "Beware abused child, you will always test the one you love for abuse. If they will abuse you and you accept it, then you become the silent abuser! I thought self-love required no test of worth! I thought love was supposed to free one and not enslave!" Check your body' reactions as you speak these self affirmations below.

- I will construct every sentence, without making a person, a place, a circumstance, or an event wrong! I will retrieve every thought, word, and feeling out of judgment. Most of all, I will not judge myself. If that person is still in my field of life, then there is something I'm still learning or sharing!

- I must be careful in allowing my partner or other person, to open in their own way, in order to let the veils or secrets down! Maybe I will be surprised by their openness to love.

- My core responsibility is, when having a conversation with my partner/other; apply affirming language that allows us to decide if we can choose more open communication. The point is; I must not feed into my partner's, friend or family's issues without, first being aware of my own needs, wants, and desires, first.

"I now know that the relationship I have with my partner mirrors the one with my dad/mom, my own inner female/male arguments, as well as the Divine mother/father parent within. My integrity in communication is a measure of my own self-awareness; all the places I can give and receive love equally."

Example: "I know you might feel that I've abandoned you, but I'm confused, and want to create a space in our relationship to be safe enough to discuss our needs so we can both have what we want without hurting each other!"

This shows equality, respect, and allows the other to change and grow in the very moment of that exchange! I have come a long way. Love is simple when self honesty and self trust guide me." After all, isn't this exactly the same inner dialogue you would have in prayer/meditation with your own soul spirit?

What will happen to our children on the new Earth?

Will their DNA be more evolved?

How do they really learn?

ARTICLE

Children Teach Us About the Science of Love: When children are connected to their imagination, then they live through their soul and spirit. Their ego is warranted in its request and they trust to give to life and receive from the Presence of life. One of the greatest brain drains in human education is to make learning a linear mental process of the neo cortex monkey brain. The science of Love is the same as the science of learning. Learning is really an emotionally based triggering system in the neural chemical brain synapses and in the neural heart. Children's brains are wired to trust one self to give to live and to receive from life.

This bonding with life allows the child to create and express at any given moment from their impassioned imagination. This way they can't be thrown out of their own external reality. They are inner directed and have emotional dominion and can take charge of their joy. They are in touch with their genius and soul's purpose. This is the divine right of every being.

This in turn re-programs the ancestral parental DNA they inherit from their parents. It takes the form of negative thoughts, feelings, attitudes, and beliefs in the brain. Their bodies are able to adapt genetic repairs quite naturally, once they clear the family of origin's negative programs. This is a natural form of genetic splicing coded in their DNA and is the access point to their genius. Previous generations have coded it out of their DNA through chronic abuse. In the past it only took three generations to change the DNA programming. This has been recoded in our DNA by these children.

So, we begin as children. We learn to parent ourselves wholly, and then return to unlimited freedom of being a child again, but without distortion. One learns to be what they already are and to be their own authority. That is the natural and evolving nature of self-love in its expressive creativity or in the heart of the imagination. This imagination is called: consciousness, intuition, knowing, inner direction, God within, Holy Presence/Spirit, life force, or a directed focus of following inner desire focused through the heart's intent. The super conscious brain teaches us that the brain acts as a conscious computer (crystalline), imaging processing device that can access distorted and negative DNA experience and decode it, from the lower cerebellum, while accessing pure uncontaminated memory from the pineal and pituitary glands. This human angel computer is utilized to create and experience something that the human form has never evolved to. So learning has very little to do with the mind.

Learning is based on emotional dominion. When a child no longer has to process the programs of the past family DNA, or has to seek pleasure in a future fantasy, then the child is in the ever-present moment. If the child is in the past, they are most concerned with fears of what mother will say or do about their bed-wetting or if they are worthy to carry mom's fears for her in order to be loved. Perhaps they are concerned about father's drinking problem. In response, the burdened child is excited to get home and watch cartoons or fantasy on Star Trek, which is a future event. Here, the child is driven out of his moment and own experience. His brain keeps miss-firing the DNA or mother bonding gene code so he doesn't feel bonded with this first mother principle of love.

Therefore, his father bonded RNA gene must also misfire, and any creative imagination is limited by the lack of bonding to his own love.

Learning must be inner directed. It is in that moment of connection to self, that any desired learning is self directed from the child's own DNA brain purity. Any learning experience should allow the child to be the movie and the moviemaker at the same time. The experience comes from the child's own authority as it is directed by the soul of the child and can be immediately owned into understanding and wisdom without the impediment of judgment. This allows the super-conscious brain to take over. External guidance only serves to help exploration and problem solving in the real world as the child is allowed to be his own teacher. This allows for maximum freedom in learning.

Special education has been the map maker in understanding how the brain works. These children have taught us that there is an RNA-DNA code that naturally knows how to access all modalities of the brain simultaneously. However, event memory of person, place, circumstance, and time, can hold the past crystallized thought forms in the neo-cortex, unless the child is allowed permission to dismiss the program of the genetic parents and does not have to carry it. The ego is released from being directed by the neo-cortex and therefore can be under the guidance of the midbrain or psychic knowing of the higher brain centers.

This allows for the creation of new thoughts, which in turn unplug thoughts or images of the past that centered on protection of the organism: security, war, success, and old dreams. New thoughts will allow new dreams to collapse into matter. That which is unknown can be known from bringing the future into the "now brain" through image messages sent through new neuron-nets, as the censors of the past are no longer in control. The old programs have served as teacher until new imagination is stimulated by the natural laws of our first primal emotion; that of focused desire that governs self love. In the ever-present moment, not seduced into the past or future, is the focused freedom to create into form, from energy, something; a plan, or idea. In quantum physics this is called "zero point." This meeting space is just at the zero point speed of light between matter and anti-matter.

It is not dependent on person, place, circumstance, or event, which allows all possibilities to be considered in the electron of choice, leaving a clear moment for a new energy to be lowered into mass from the soul of the dreamer.

This consciousness is a new thought, feeling, or attitude that keeps the personality enjoying the sums of its experience rather than fighting life. The energy of the overall attitude is sent in rapid speed to the brain and returns in matter as a thing or experience. This is quantum physics at its best and children do it naturally.

The personality slowly comes under the dominion of the DNA's inner direction, as the knowing brain searches for new experience based on emotionally based data that offer clear and pure interpretations, based on the free will of the exploring child. If there is a misfiring into the past, the brain can self correct by bringing the child back to the present moment through intended focus. It takes 7 to 21 old earth days of consistent focus to change a habitual neuron-net pattern in the brain.

The teacher offers the child baseline information. The child uses that data to teach himself whatever is required to satisfy his adventure, thus eliminating external controls that have kept education about the mind, rather than a multi-sensory experience. Learning becomes an inner directed process, rather than a simulated synthetic or external experience. The hypnotic effects of reality or fantasy are never attractive to children who begin to discover that they have worlds within them to discover that are only stimulated by an outer playful match. It is important to now understand how quantum learning does occur in the higher cycling brain centers.

The brain weighs about three pounds and contains 100 billion nerve cells. This is the same number of stars that exist in the Milky Way. Each nerve cell has between 1000 and 10,000 connections with other nerve cells. So what children know are what atomic and subatomic particles know; that all time and space converge in their single moments of play from a vast array of toys. In that moment, they are time and space. Here all life, all love, all consciousness exists on the point of a pin; a creative passionate exploration of a simple desire to know more about the reflection of the self, through experience.

Essentially, children learn through inner-directed consciousness, which is based on wave frequency imaging. This means that the light tubes around the neurons store photonic light codes of information in quantum fields of wave energy. When a light, color, or sound wave is perceived or interrupted, through a chosen desired focus, then something new is learned. The child draws in information from holographic images from light waves that store all the Known and Unknown. All information is stored in these waves, rather than the brain. This is the big bang over and over again; tapping into holographic information. These wave band portals are accessed through desire.

<u>**So our brain communicates**</u> to us with words, images, and chemical impulses through the free will choice to bring thought patterns into a three-dimensional reality. This is an actual image of any given subjective perception creating a coherent light pattern. This is standard field theory. A wave form is only individuated when there is a search for something new. It is like pulling information out of a vast universal library based on a perceived thought, feeling, attitude, belief, intention, commitment, choice, word, or action.

The child uses a subjective experience to validate a truth viewpoint.

<u>**Intuition happens,**</u> when the perception and the object image agree or meet; like a mirror in a converging wave form, where thought patterns meet and greet, or like a discovery made in a type of book of knowledge. There is an inner knowing that answers any question or desire that already exists. That knowing acts like a scanning device to internet the light arrays that will answer the question. Phase, amplitude, and frequency dictate the quality and quantity of the learning desired as measured by human: thought, attitude and belief intensities, both negative and positive.

Lofty thoughts excite the spirit DNA knowledge. Polarity emotions affect the soul blueprints, and survival needs effect human feelings. The greater the focus on thoughts coming from the higher physic brain centers, the more knowledge available for joyous creations.

<u>**Passion, desire, instinct, or a contemplative fixation,**</u> ignites wave interpretation, or a set of neural thought patterns in the DNA, into a natural state of continual co-creation. Again the wave form holography simply creates a specific pattern of information to be studied by the brain, the whole body, and its chemicals.

The largest wisdom is that we are each other, and we enter the field of love. We can merge, walk through each other, or leave. When we can absorb love in the world of matter, we can return to love in the world of energy. It is consciousness within all life that seeks to come to know itself as this love. This is the same purity and innocence that children and every life form are born with. This pure simple knowing of the innocent child is the greatest natural resource of mankind. Yet, the prostitution of their DNA innocence levels has set the evolution of this planet back 500,000 years. It is being slowly redeemed by the super-psychic quantum children who bask in a pure intention of direct access to the higher frequency fields of love, at all times. These crystal children can grow themselves directly through thought, rather than biochemistry.

The emotional field of the quantum child understands the heart as one big pulsating field where rocks, plants, animals, people, atoms, particles, waves, all are in continual communication and that we are always moving through each other. Until we understand how love and light work, in a gravity field of bi-photons, or polarity resolution of emotions; then how we are able to accept unconditional love that moves beyond the speed of light? Until then we will be the consumers of life, and false technologies, rather than the Gods of life that we truly are.

Children are born knowing this until the global collective forces them to give it up. This is what the science of love is seeking to discover in its respect for life. Soon the globe will discover, that in the world of matter, we can copy and transfer magnetic signatures from our DNA cells to signature radiant health, emotional harmony, or manifestation of our food and needs.

Again, we are back to thoughts, feelings, attitudes and beliefs. We magnetize to ourselves, exactly what we are at any given moment. This physical world is the one we must love as ourselves, and the quantum child is our teacher. The ancients have tried pass on to this knowing that was in each human spirit. Most of us have given our power balance away to teachers, governments, and religions; to dependencies or addictions, and failed to look within to find the God truth of our very being. The children will love us back into ourselves, if only we will let them.

How do we create using the superconscious or physic brain? Are miracles natural?

ARTICLE- **The Art of Manifestation and Precipitation:**
Communication of a desired request to manifest depends on the relationship with your higher self. Are you your Holy Spirit? Are you able to create imaging in your brain through coming to a still point and breathing your desire into your own movie on your frontal lobe, since this is the part of the brain that controls imaging from the DNA? Your request is time variant depending on any delay in communication time with the inner self, (soul spirit). Your inner voice of clarity is dependant on the completion of negative thoughts, feelings, attitudes, or beliefs, and of altered ego/reactive patterns of the past.

The quality and intensity of emotion dictates the result. The more passionate is the imagination, and the less limited emotion, the quicker the manifest. Are you sending out signals or messages from the old neo-cortex monkey brain or the god-self psychic brain?
If the psychic energy band infrared frequencies are not firing on a consistent level, then one must surrender control, to the Holy Spirit in order to bring changes through recycling more negative emotional reactions which can over- ride any old brain patterns of past programming, such as: "I'm not worthy, women can't create what they want, or men must be aggressive." The brain chemistry cycling is still lagging at 8.4 cycles per second instead of the desired 11.7 midbrain connection.

Love is a basic principle of manifestation. Love does not mean something must be given or taken. It does not mean abuse, accommodation, or obliteration. Unconditional love is receiving/giving equally, the right to commit to choices, the right to identity as a unique expression, and an intimate communion with one's spirit. One simply pulls from the DNA blueprints claimed from the wisdom mastered in soul's evolution. This re-opens access to the memory stored in the original spirit blueprints as well.

Manifestation has to do with things visible, that already exist and involves time: cars, homes, and so on. The neo-cortex, which is solution oriented in thought, must be by passed in order to reach the midbrain. The more one is free from the limited thought or social consciousness of persons, places, circumstances, or events; the quicker the manifestation. When the progression of feelings moves from expectancy, knowing, and then being, there is a birth of a desired focus. One knows that their spirit supports their desire in the Presence of all life. The being state requires that one images the desire as if the whole body is experiencing it in the now.

Whatever you focus on and pour your life energy into produces your reality, your destiny, and your future. The attitude of the inner self must be in total agreement with soul's agenda and/or spirit's overall DNA plan for the perfect action/object/desired image to manifest in the outer world. One images the desire on the brain by imagining its touch, taste, smell, cellular feel, vision, embodying a full flavored knowingness and brings it into the present now moment. It then becomes the law in one's experience.

Precipitation has to do with the non-visible and does not involve time. Love collapses time and brings into existence new creations through emotions of higher frequencies, that before, did not exist. This takes place in the midbrain where one is free from attachment and reactive emotion. This greater love flow then passes through the body outward to harmonize the outer frequency signals, to match the heart's higher frequency desire. The brain wiring must fire from the neo-cortex to the lower cerebellum. This is the seat of Divine memory for every life form.

If psychic or infrared mid-brain frequency is consistent, a minimum of 11.7 cycles per second, then breath takes one into the Void, or creation chamber. There is no thought, no feeling, no agenda, no attachment, no doubt, no time. The inner attitude must include unconditional love so the energy is free and without opposition. The desire then becomes law. In this state, one's whole becomes the desire instantly. The human Spirit gets to experience what it knows itself to be, in desire. The object is breathed into being. The image that was drawn up from the frontal lobe imprint enters physicality and/or time.

I Am, Where I is God and Am is Law, allows the power and the precipitation of that which I desire to create. The object desired and the experience desired, become one with you as creator. There is no thing that you can't command dominion over, when the Higher Self is fully integrated in the biology including: controlling the elements of weather, healing the Earth, instant body healing, or any other gift stored in the abilities and gifts blueprint of the DNA.

A List of Some of the Holy Spirit Gifts to Inspire:

- To manifest or de-manifest the body
- The ability to levitate or fly
- The ability to know anything on command
- The ability to communicate with beings from other realities beyond the physical
- To create objects from pure energy
- To Move objects with one's thoughts
- The ability to teleport or bi-locate
- To love all life unconditionally
- To precipitate gold or diamonds

How will our human character aspects change or replace wounds in our DNA, on the new Earth?

ARTICLE- *Living without Your Old Story*
Can You Live Without Telling Your Old Story Over and Over, and re-imprinting it in your brain? Limitations hold onto; a guaranteed outcome, to the fear of taking risks, and to the avoidance of an experience that is outside of control. Freedom is about total and absolute trust in yourself and the ability to take charge of your joy by being your own sovereign authority. The overall experience on any given day is the accumulation of all your negative and positive thoughts and feelings. Does your energy output result in hate, judgment, blame, shame, doubt, regret, obsessive thought, fear, rage? Does addiction consume you?

Choosing from the list below:

- How many positive character emotions does it take to rebalance your intake energy for your giving/receiving quotient of loving?
- Are you still suffering from the spiritual depression described in the following list of words?

*Accepting * Allowing *unconditional *Balanced *Caring *Changing *Clear *Complete *Actualizing *Solution oriented *Flexible *Spontaneous *Resourceful *Conscious * Creative *Curious *Interdependent *Expansive *Laughter *Detachment *Imaginative *Trusting *Discerning *Ecstatic *Empowered *Adaptable *Engaging *Ever-present *Determined *Adaptable *Harmonious *Excellent *Expectant independent strong *Fluid *Free *Hopeful *Playful *Humorous *Inner connected *Inner guided *Resonant *Organized *Tenacious *Enduring *Inspirational *Inventive *Joyous *Knowing *Light *Growing *Magnificent * Non-reactive *Compassionate

*Satisfied *Confident *Passionate *Perfect *Pleased * Self Aware *Self-assured *Cooperative *Self-realized *Self-reflective *Sovereign *Splendid *Supportive *Unified *Unlimited

Spiritual depression:

This type of depression is often called the dark night of the soul. This is the result of our trying to keep energy in the lower three seals of the pelvis, stomach, and solar plexus. When our thoughts and feelings are stuck in: survival and sexuality (1st seal); sickness, worthiness and esteem (2nd seal); and power, control and victimization (3rd seal), the sexual, or life force energy, is trying to move up and be fed by the higher brain centers to heal. We need to surrender, relax and let go of the need to control everything and trust that our Spirit will take care of us. Our Spirit never brings anything to us that we cannot handle in order to resolve a belief or feeling still remaining on the soul's agenda so that the energy can return to you. We teach ourselves with feelings and beliefs. Can you ask your Spirit for Its strength to get you through this, knowing that the body knows how to naturally heal itself when it lets go the past?

Is the integration of male and female emotions required to merge the twin soul and the twin spirit bodies?

ARTICLE-*Soul Gender Bodies*

We choose and are magnetically drawn into bodies so that we can gain the most learning in any given lifetime role and balance any judgments. Often times male soul energies will choose female bodies for the balancing. Often female soul energies will choose male bodies to balance and go beyond gender and balance soul or spirit family lessons.

The Major judgment made by soul spirit families was on the experiences of separation into polarity: male/female, dark/light, matter/spirit, female DNA emotion /male RNA emotion. Since the soul spirit was designed to process the DNA/RNA through the emotion of love, this balance of male and female emotions is a main key to resolving all Earth duality in the human experience.

We remember our inner male and female through their gifts and their wounds. This allows us to close out time lines (holograms) that otherwise might never be resolved.

One most certainly does not need to repeat an 1859 lifetime of survival, disease, and betrayal; or the memory of the loss of one's home planet, over and over, in one's cell memory! We choose many lifetimes in order to balance our male and female energies and bring them into harmony in this current time. It was the unnecessary repetition of negative patterns of limitation, lifetime after lifetime, that have made our old Earth stories alter the memory of love in our DNA/RNA, forgetting that we are all sparks of Creation.

Accessing Male and Female Emotions

Each one of us carries the energy and emotions of both male and female regardless of gender. The female represents home, hearth, children, heart, bonding, unconditional love, relationship, and partnership. She must express her feelings and her creativity. She will feel a vast range of positive and negative emotions and come back to love, knowing that her love protects all emotions. She makes all experiences safe, protecting the right to life and free will. She is the heart of the imagination.

The male nurtures, supports, and is in service to the female creations. His nature is manifestation, time, form building, architecture, movement, protection, maintenance, problem solving, boundaries, mind, and the preservation of life. His domain is the external reality and its forms, structures, and functions know all actions are sacred.

The soul records male soul and female soul experiences, which are stored in the subconscious memory of the body you are now in. Use your imagination to feel yourself in the male body or the female body sensing and observing the experience like you is watching a story. How did that parallel self feel about them self, their relationship, their profession, and the society or time line they were drawn into by birth? Let them tell you their story. Each time you use this exercise, it serves as a life review and allows for higher vibration energy patterns to be activated and remembered in the DNA.

Going Beyond Gender:
Inner Dialogue of a Typical Woman talking to her Male/female Selves:
"When I was in a male body I wanted to give love to my female parallel self. When I was in a female body, I wanted to give love to my male parallel self. I had many lifetimes where this wasn't possible. I was always looking to reunite my twin selves. I also had lifetimes where I felt this emotionally, mentally, physically, and spiritually in varying degrees, but never solidly all in one body. I had to have a relationship with another to accomplish this.
I often sought to find this in wounded relationships. I would have someone love me more than I loved them! I experienced: jealousy, abuse, pain, rejection, abandonment, hurt, rage, and all human emotions trying to configure a relationship without being trapped, or just fitting in to cultural, social, political, or gender role. All this seemed to be at the price of personal love. Impersonal love was something that only belonged to spirit lifetimes. I wanted to experience love in this body!

Often my relationship addictions in those lifetimes felt like it was based on animal feelings, not warm and tender love. I felt dependence and attachment like it was a disorder. This feels like charged passion based on millions of years of an addictive neuron-chemical morphine drip of: fear, abuse, hurt, abandonment and abject and utter loneliness; the dark night of the soul. I knew it could not be the natural emotions of a free spirit. I was thrown into the dilemma of a maybe. Maybe I'm supposed to be my own the perfect partner inside first, but how do you do that without a partner for reflection?

I have this increasingly greater relationship with the balance of my male and female self in this modern age. Even now, I feel the depth of my emotions arise: the utter, anger and grief and disappointment that are coming from my body cells. This, not feeling loved, feels overwhelming. I was counting on feeling an equal relationship in passion, respect and creative purpose together! I will make a new agreement with myself.

I know that if I don't, my cells will die; my body will die, without this love. My grief and anger must not overwhelm my cells. I will move forward into my own truth of my own soul. I know my soul weighs 13 ounces and sits in the right heart chamber. I don't have to abandon my human male or female self to appease my spirit. I know the other aspects of self at higher frequencies don't have cellular bodies. They need to translate the information from my biology to understand that I'm done with these painful lessons and I want to live in my body and my soul, so my spirit can rebirth inside me. Then I know all my aspects are healed. I realize that my spirit has become my inner lover is feeding the relationship deep within me that I may share it and be nurtured by it, fed by it, and share it with another."

Will my human relationships improve if i merge my inner twin?

ARTICLE- *the soul spirit twin relationship- the inetegration of inner male and female emotion*

Most communication in your relationships is with your inner twin. This, your male/female self, is directly mirrored in your partnered relationships and marriages. Problems can be avoided when there is an understanding that the female DNA emotions & male DNA emotions have different character attributes of feelings and functions. These strands in our genetic profiles produce different qualities of emotions which must be merged and blended. This is of primal importance since the female **DNA (pineal gland)** leads in love and compassion and the male **RNA (pituitary gland)** interprets this information into actions of physical form. In fact, the male body is wired to die if he can't serve this love and manifest from it. That is why he is always looking for the female reflection within himself.

Problems arise when the female expects the male to feel exactly the same way she does or vice versa. He cannot, because he experiences what she experiences through a different quality in his male emotion. It is much like translating her English to Spanish and back into his English! You created male and female precisely to experience the differences in emotions, in order to merge both emotions in partnership, without losing the unique expression of either partner. In other words; "I do not know who you are if I can not feel you or I AM in you and You are in Me!"

The bonus; was to be: two humans, or two soul spirits, or two soul spirits; moving in and out of each other as One, so the mirror reflection of love would provide a fail safe against the feeling of being alone, separate, and away from home! You must take the time to listen to the feelings of your partner and reflect on what those feelings mean inside you so you can continually be in open agreements and dialogue for your shared soul purpose, with each mutual creation, being like a new born child.

<u>Example</u>: If you are both trying to manifest abundance, then she might feel her worth in terms of the amount of shared intimate times together. He might feel the same worth as to whether or not he can provide the focus, time, energy, and power connections to manifest her dreams, or face possible failure.

<u>Both still must feel their own inner interpretation of worth,</u> because it was not natural for them to argue or compete for their worth. Also the degree to which both are in touch with their very own inner male and female emotion, directly affects the speed of their desired dream to arrive. Very often, one partner may be trying to carry their partner's male or female energy for them, creating an imbalance. If both partners are drowning in too much negative emotion or too much female, then paralysis will result. On the other hand, if both are doing just to avoid feeling or too much male, then the reflection for inner creating is lost! They must each merge their own worth without judging the feelings of the other!

<u>The Importance of the Balance of Inner Male and Female Emotions:</u>
As you read about both male and female emotions in the section below, notice the balance the merge you keep inside you own female DNA and male RNA emotions. Notice how their balance spills over into your outer relatedness. And remember, this spills over onto the relationships you have with all the systems on your planet such as your governments, churches, schools, and communities, since you are the parents and leaders of the new Earth. To be a good steward of Earth, you must be a good steward of compassionate and equal ways of relating and respect for each others' love. Many women have brought in more male soul energy into their female body, and many men have brought in more female energy into their male body, for the purpose of clearing soul trauma around the twin separations, so that the spirit can further merge in the body.

<u>FEMALE EMOTION:</u> She cycles all emotions through earth; (human love) air; (soul purpose) fire; (creational passion); water, (love) and ether (spirit). She represents home, hearth, children, heart, bonding to life, unconditional love, equal relationship and partnership. She must express her feelings, her creativity and feels a vast range of positive and negative emotions, reflected by her mate; which all return to protection under love. Her overall feeling tones are softer, tendered, quieter, and passionately subtle. She protects the original right to life and free will. She is the heart of the imagination and her desires are raw, primordial, and instinctual, as her will rides natural law. The conscious void is her womb space, the birthplace of her creativity and the focus of her love. She is the healed woman-God of Earth and bonded in sisterhood with all women.

Negative Female Emotion:
She is focused on dark and heavy emotions, which replace sisterhood and bonding. She will abandon abuse and use her children for her own needs. She will compete with other females for power, or try to devour or kill her own partner if he threatens to abuse her. She is subject to the negative altered-ego as the collective unconscious where pain, shame, blame, judgment and suffering predominate. She destroys in violence rather than recycle in the natural order.

Violence replaces natural cycles as orgasms, volcanoes, and birth become violent. Sexual fantasy replaces imagination, the Divine, and the ecstatic bliss body.

Enmeshment: physical, sexual, mental, emotional replace bonding. She feels not enough as a woman and will hide in the Void, sometimes withdrawing the life force and going into involution or further into Black Hole. She will go into attack and defend as a standard defense. Here she questions whether or not she can hold her own love. She feels banished, parched, and forced into the underworld in sacrifice.

Her war with the male is always over the fact that he took prime role as Creator and in the creational merge. She struggles to understand the very male emotion she has agreed to carry in the Divine DNA belly of her creations. Sacrifice has replaced sacred living; fear has replaced imagination and Divine desire. Worst of all, she feels the pressure of the male RNA helix to gain control of all the genetic bloodlines, which by law is her natural function. She experiences male anger, rage, and violence for the first time and feels abandoned, betrayed, and unsupported by the other half of her Soul-Spirit.

She had accepted the male genetics in order to sustain a body. In reality, her inexperience, judgment, and fear created a foreign ruler, although Cosmic Law says that all experience is by agreement, and that there is no violation in any reality.

Male Emotion: He nurtures, supports, and is in service to the female's desired creations through manifestation, time, form building, architecture, movement, protection, maintenance, problem solving, boundaries, mind, and the preservation of life. He is bonded in brotherhood with all men.

All actions and experiences are gained through the primary emotions of recognition and acceptance for providing for her needs; her home and her bloodline creations, and her love focus. He has the same expression of a wide range of all emotions, male creativity and expression as well; but all is desolate unless he can merge with her and play his role in service to her. Also, the overall feeling tones are stronger, harder, more intense with outward motion, and he always seeks to please the female. Although he feels he does not always understand her different feeling tones; he respects them and feels them in his own way. The music and light patterns in the language of his RNA are different. He is the healed man-God of Earth!

Negative Male Emotion:

His emotional reactions are expressed in: abuse, rage, anger, violence, control, blame, and shame, as a defense against the creative power of the female. He will kill her or her children unless they fit into his forms or ideas. He lives outside his emotions and expects the female to carry their expression for him. He greatly fears the Void and that he will be castrated in the Great Abyss and cease to be. He competes and wars with other creator males, for control of the universe. He is subject to the negative altered-ego and collective unconscious beliefs that he created.

Power without love, postures in a false ego that fosters pure male will without adaptation and change, even to the point of cutting off or altering the Divine DNA love blueprint. Here, creating becomes more important than loving and sharing. He will force the other half of himself, to lose evolution or hide in the Void if absolute control is needed. Here anger, rage, violence, and fear predominate as male emotions, rather than allowing any vulnerability or wounded-ness. These emotions then become confused as a true focus of love. He must keep the female as second principle of creation to remain in control. This could be called reverse polarization. Power replaces a divine love focus and love is conditional. Love is often a synthetic experience of technology as an avoidance of the experience of true direct emotions.

The true male matrix has accepted female genetics in order to sustain a form within heart. His inexperience, judgment, and fear had propelled him into a forced state of addictive power. There is no violation in any reality since all experience is agreed on to gain resolution and wisdom. This was an agreed choice by Soul-Spirit with the female matrix as well.

Therefore, remember to balance your inner male/female at each cycle of change, no matter what body you are in, so as to draw in the perfect relationships you most desire to experience in greater love. This personal merge will keep all other systems on your new planet merged with the new universe you are creating! Neither twin must ever believe that they have to compete for their worth, their joy, self expression, or creative love ever again. They must re-merge in their return home, ever enhancing creation with more love! Read this true twin story.

WHY IS THE PLANETARY MALE ENERGY SO IMBALANCED?

ARTICLE - Male Identity Crisis-The Return of Male Instinct
The planetary male is in an identity crisis. Many women are complaining that they are tired of carrying their partner's emotions for him and that he has to do his own feeling or his own inner homework. The male will say that he has no idea what she means and that, "his job is to protect, preserve, and provide for the family, and that, is how he feels." Women complain that their children act out the hidden emotions in the marriage when the mate communication breaks down. Women, all over the world, wonder when the distorted male will stop trying to control, his or is mate's worth, with his anger. They pray that their men and governments will stop warring and tearing their families apart and killing their children. Many women across the world are amazed that their governments in the United Nations still allow genocide, rape, and starvation onto death, with the excuse of wars of terror! Is it the inner or outer terrorist that rules their planet?

If you're having trouble with relationships, don't panic! The males are feeling their own intuitive and emotional connection, while the females are feeing their own physical and mental connection to merge the hemispheres of their male-female brain. Although, mirroring this process through another is acceptable, it still must be done inside each human heart and vehicle, in order that each has an inner identity communication with their individual soul spirit! This wonderful flavor of owning one's feelings in equal identity emotion adds a great sense of self worth, equal expression, and conscious responsibility in relatedness.

The Divine, wired the male body to live his function as: protector, provider and preserver. When the male RNA was ruptured through the distortion of judgment that love could be lost in the separation of the twin energies, the male was forced to trade off **his instinct** to love for feelings of competition, war, abuse, and rage. Cut off from his female, he felt as if she didn't exist or that he would die without the identity connection to her feelings thereby, loosing his true purpose in service to manifest whatever they desired as one love. In loosing his natural instinct to feel each other as one spirit, he felt they could no longer literally re-create the other, should they be lost in the cosmos; that the DNA could no longer replicate the RNA and vice versa, need be! Now he could be drawn into war to fight for his mate or compete with another male to find a surrogate. Being split apart, they both begin to feel things that angels were never intended to feel in substitution for love: the stealing of love from another, the stealing of love from another's mate; the stealing of love from one's own creations. These unnatural emotions, caused by the choices to reject the naturalness of love, produced unnatural and unspeakable acts in the DNA love gene: war sexual abuse, control, terror, and self hatred of one's own spirit.

So women of the world, help your mate to feel and identify his own emotions by listening and helping him trust the feelings in his body and his heart. Giving him the language of emotion is akin to giving him the language of love so natural to the female brain. Help him understand that his harder feelings of rage, anger, fear, and control, can be loved, if he allows himself to feel each emotion all the way through to his heart, without cutting it off, or shutting it down in his body, he will end up in his heart. In that place is the communication with his partner, his inner twin spirit, and the creative solutions for life and unlimited provision. When sharing and loving with equal respect for emotions, the energy can rise up from the lower body into the heart and ignite brain cells from both his male and female intuition. This way he realizes that both partners can have their dreams met, or even shared, in a relationship, and that he has not failed in his role. Note that the quality of his feelings may be different, with more of a focus on: acceptance/ rejection, success/ failures in serving the female to manifest her home in the structures and materiality of the physical world. The divine female quality of emotion is centered on softer feelings of home, hearth, children, and the loyalty of her partner's love. Both partners must find both qualities of these emotions within their own hearts and bodies now. The age old argument of who is in charge of the emotions, who is in charge of the worth, or who is in charge of the purpose, can rest, and love can be restored in its natural divine compliment.

The Divine chose the male DNA and RNA to enjoy these wonderful differences so that love could grow and endure change in both the physical and non physical realms! When the inner partner and the outer partner are sharing their feelings, their worth, and their purpose; then their desires are answered to in abundance.Collective memory healing is the restoration of the inner and outer heart spirit function in the male principle. Now that the soul of the goddess has returned, she has restored the bonding agent of love, compassion, and understanding itself. In holding that love, she re-creates her mates feeling heart, when he seems he has lost his way from love. She does this, by re-connecting him to his instinctual male feelings so he can let his body cry, feel, and trust his heart in order that both can operate in service to ONE soul and spirit purpose again. The old male collective unconscious is feeling, yet resisting, the re- balancing of the love of the scared masculine in all the male dominated systems on the planet, in the human male body, and every aspect of human relationships. This balance in your planetary healing is crucial to the return of all life as being a part of the ONE LOVE and living in unity upon the planet. The male body is no longer able to hide its feelings, so now many male emotions just spit out of the body like a volcano, or get acted out inappropriately, accounting for many seeming heinous acts. Be patient as this burden upon the old Earth male, to be programmed to hide or not understand his true feelings is lifted off the planet, and goes out to the rest of the universe to heal itself from the false perception that Source love could be somehow torn apart by the illusion of experience.

This wonderful twin flame story /channeling, gives you a full experience of the twin flame merge:

Jayne Chilkes and Her Twin Flame: *http://theangelschannel.netfirms.com*

Part One

Thank you thank you thank you for we are to begin our adventure. Long, long ago there was a beautiful princess and she had long golden locks and glorious fair skin. Her robes were of silk and gold and she glided into the room as if she had wings. I, the Prince, was so enamored by her. We were blissfully in love and in adoration of every thought and every gesture. We were inseparable. We were not possessive, nor jealous. We were in perfect harmony and unconditional in our approach. I wanted what would make her happy, and she wanted what would make me happy. We would often fantasize about travel to foreign lands and to have adventures together or apart. We always planned to come back to one another after our travels to share more delights. And this is what we always did. It was a promise between us. We would travel through the eyes of others too. We could do that because we were so light.

I watched the world through a Mongolian, an American Indian Chief, a Zulu warrior, a Rastafarian, a rich American Banker, a French Priest, an Astronomer, a Navy Captain and many more. My beloved Princess traveled too - she drifted from Sirius to Egypt, from Japan to China, to Bali and England. She had many English lives from medieval times to now. She always held on to her spirituality and chose delicate female orientated souls. I always chose souls that were forceful and had leadership qualities. Between our travels we would return to our dwelling on Sharkti, where we shared our journeys. Sometimes she stayed behind and sometimes I did. This time I did. She needed the experience one last time and I said I would complete our journeys here in my position in soul. I will evaluate our position and refrain from travel. I decided to travel through frequencies of higher dimensions and consolidate our position together. This is because this is her time to clear all our journeys emotional dross. She is clearing all mine and hers as she is in the emotional field of mother earth. Once she has done this, and she is close now, she will be set free to reside in all our dimensions at once. I am waiting for my Princess to return and for her to say our work is done.

I have had many realizations in the higher dimensions. I am a child of God and all that that entails. I have the power that God bestowed upon His/Her children. I evaluate from my highest position and most powerful in terms of Love and Light where my energy should be distributed and how.

Through the physical body of my Princess I charge her with this energy to place it correctly in ways her human mind does not comprehend. She becomes a conduit to apply love and light on mother earth and its inhabitants. Her human mind does not need to grasp this concept or the concept that Twin Flames can be or do anything within the Laws of the Universe. They can set up Light Domes, Light Planets, Light Fields, Light Portals, and Light Universes if they so choose. I speak to all of those knowing or awaiting their Beloved Twin Flame, grasp the moment, take your power back to self and know your entitlement. More rapidly than ever before we are entitled to flow from higher to lower in octave or frequency. Yet the lower dimensions does not mean dense, necessarily, just more of an experiential level of adjusting mental, emotional, spiritual planes simultaneously. The vastness of knowledge acquired in one lifetime on earth will or could see you to a quicker ascension than that of a lifetime on any other planet in the universe! Your material world holds treasures of free will way beyond the comprehension of many. Thus even when you are quiet and nothing seems to be happening you are readjusting all levels of your being readying yourself for the next nugget of information, adventure, levels of ascension and so forth.

Twin flame Adventures

One of my strangest adventures was when I became an Arcturian Leader and Warrior. Here we were trained to be a fighter to the end. We were relentless in keeping our empire pristine without any invaders from nearby planets. We were very proud of being Arcturians and very kind but firm. In fact we were rigid in our opinions and defiant in the upkeep of our Empire. So I stood a formidable being, defending my planet. Unbeknown to my consciousness that my beloved Princess was waiting for my return.

I did not return at the correct time and held off my return for several other lifetimes. My Princess as unconditional as she was had had lifetimes that had tampered with her purity and judgment. She felt abandoned, hurt and sad. We were now becoming conditional and found that to keep our original plan was more and more challenging. To wipe the tears of my beloved, I knew our adventures had to continue and we would meet less and less. In fact our memory got almost obliterated through time. Still though our higher selves were in tact. It was only when we realized that our journeys and adventures on other planets including earth were finally turning full circle could we register forgiveness and unconditionally once more.

Perhaps to the human this was sad, yet to us the experience was our ultimate savior and we knew we could achieve our original position together when the time was right. And indeed there has been a healing of this memory with forgiveness.

Another adventure of mine, I was a great poet and writer of my day. I grew in notoriety and became the most talked about gay author in town! I was certainly the most camp and confident. Sarcasm ruled my wit, and decadence ruled my sensibility. I forgot what it was to be a Gentleman, rather a rogue of nuance and verb. For me women were untouchable, beautiful and out of my reach. Yet in return for all my dallying man spat in my face and flailed my heart. My experience thwarted by persecution I returned to soul a broken man. This I knew to be my last dramatic appearance and I went out with style! Yet defying all odds my beloved Princess returned to me and whispered in my ear "I will return to earth to experience one more lifetime to clear our past and set each other free. This I do for you and for me, for to return to our sacredness is all that truly matters." And this she has done for me, my dear Princess.

Another time, I was a French Monk. Indeed I loved to write the scriptures, day in and day out. I was in service so closely with God. I rejoiced at dawn and dusk in the name of God and His Angels. I vowed to be obedient and silent for many of those years. I was not allowed to think of my beloved yet I knew in my heart there was a great love for me. I put this down to Divine Mother. I think I understood from that happy simple life, a sense of humility that I needed to learn.

For so many lives were bold and courageous with male ego pride. I remember seeing a beautiful painting of an angel, she had long golden locks and she looked so familiar. Yet who was she and how did I know her? I was not allowed to long for her or think of her. She just lived in my heart and her Love kept me content. I knew I would meet her again one day, I just knew it.

Another situation that I need to reveal to you is way before Lemuria we resided in another time frame and galaxy. We were not human in appearance nor did we have the human experience. You and I were one, neither male nor female. We resided mainly on a planet pronounced in your language Phylamandra. We were Light and Sound and pure unadulterated Love. We enjoyed long, as in hundreds of your years, lifetimes. Other beings from outer planets corrupted our peace and beauty and little survived of the Paradise we once lived in. We saw the rise and fall of communities and many destroyed.

During this cycle you and I did descend to ascend. We held onto twin flame knowledge as we did not separate then. It was not all a lot easier then to ascend nor did we have human bodies and complexities to contend with of separation in the physical sense. We learnt to ascend as one. We are now learning to ascend as seemingly two. The richness of our existence on Phylamandra remains embedded in our DNA.

Yet we have to realize we have never had such an experience of Ascension before and thus it is more challenging yet not impossible. Consider this, most Twin Flame couples you are aware of, are from this grouping and the beginning of all Creation.

Another life, I was a communicator on planet Saturn. I was always surrounded by masses of paperwork and I was constantly dictating news from many planets.

Saturn was the main station for information and planetary news. We had a board of governors and I was a reporter at all meetings. I loved writing so I was very happy in that role. Of course you probably wouldn't recognize me as I was very round and semi reptilian. I had fingers, long ones and I could hold two pens in one hand. I needed to, so as to write two different sentences at the same time.

Think of that! I suppose we thought of each other as looking beautiful but from a human standpoint we would be a little strange to say the least. So I learnt my writing skills there and the ability to communicate succinctly and to the point. No humor though, I so missed the humor. Everyone was so formal and serious. I learnt discipline there to add to my repertoire of skills.

Did I ever tell you this one? I was wandering the earth wondering who I could be and what I could experience. I was drawn to China and became a Mandarin sage and soothsayer. Many people came to me for advice and direction in life. I helped people to find their true purpose and God. Well one day the sweetest looking woman entered my workplace. She had jet black hair, straight and flowing down her back. She wore a pink satin dress.

She bowed as I bowed to her. Her name meant "sweet music." My heart pounded for she reminded me of you my beloved. Memories flashed by as I knew her essence and her essence recognized mine. We spent many long hours together and she offered her beautiful singing voice to heal and calm others. She played the equivalent of a mandolin so melodiously. She was a treasure. Do you remember beloved? Do you remember our happiness and reunion and the hour's laughter and joy? This experience was a reprieve, to rejoice in our loving energies in a lifetime on earth.

Another time in my higher aspect and between lives I worked with Metatron as Lord Azrael with hosts of angels. We and those fighting angelic forces have soldiered through some dark energy that lingers in the atmosphere of the grid work of earth. We continue to this day to release embedded dross that clouds the balance of earth and other planetary energies. Forces of darkness are rife in patches across the grids. As much as we build light, the darker energies persist. We are growing in numbers to activate the changes that now must take place on earth. We have called in all forces of light to be active in this metamorphic period of cleansing. We are the guardians of the light and let not fear disguise the truth that light will always win. For clarification purposes, there is indeed a conspiracy afoot in the modern western world yet despite the control that is being pursued; there will be hitches which will lead to a quick defeat. In the meantime the peacemakers will be strengthened to build the New World; world of fairness and trust.

Part Two

When we are enclosed in the physical framework and body of the human we remain locked into what we perceive as real. The reality is to be enjoyed for its beauty and its beauty in all experience. The realization, that this is a dream made up by your higher self and soul purpose, releases you from the illusion of life through human eyes. It releases you to value that which is truly real and that is that which lasts forever and a day - your soul and your union with your twin flame and god self, and ultimately god him/herself.

To fathom this is deliberately mystifying. Yet when seeking those moments of reunion from your perspective they seem so distant, so confusing, just close your eyes, quieting all thoughts and be in silence. Then listen within very hard, listen to your higher self calling you, listen for your twin calling you and listen for gods words whispering love to you. Create a journal of your findings, allow your hands to just write and see what flows when the mind does not interfere. Just as this hand is doing right now, celebrate dear friends, for this moment is the only moment that matters. Tomorrow there will be more moments to celebrate. Fears from the past shadow tomorrows. You forget the present and the great joy of being alive, ever present in the moment. Each moment is a miracle of life flowing through you, helping you to create all that you desire, wish for as you conjure up the wonder of life and gratitude for all that you are.

For you know neither who you are nor the individual soul that lies beneath the surface waiting for you to recognize your true nature. So I come back to my adventures.

Did I tell you this one? I was often peeking into others lives and sensing the areas of existence I would like to experience. I found some wonderful people in the Himalayas and I chose them as my parents. I was brought up in the mountains far away from towns. We often visited a sacred area where the masters lived. I went there every week from a very young age. I was taught the ways of the masters. I was taught that whatever you think becomes a reality in some form. So I learnt to think of positive ways to improve my life and the lives of others.

I walked with Saints, some of whom were hundreds of years old. You could almost see through them. They were real but translucent. Sometimes they would disappear before my eyes and then return a few weeks or months later. I often wondered where they went. I asked one day where did you go Brother? He was very old with a white beard and a loin cloth, with very kind eyes. "My son, I went to the Ashram in the sky. I brought back some bread and cheese to eat. Let us enjoy it together." He also brought back this sweet rice biscuit he knew I loved. "Here is your favorite," he would say. Out of nowhere the sweet rice biscuits would appear in his hand. "How did you do that?" I would wonder. "Ah, my son you will learn to do that one day, if you listen to the teachings and follow our advice." I lived there for hundreds of years. I became an old man to the young and I offered the same advice I once heard when I was young.

I lived in the Ashram in the sky and visited my Himalayan grounds often. I would always be accompanied by other Masters. I so admired them all and still do. We still can be heard if you listen carefully. I am your Master, beloved. I will clear the muddy waters if you were to just ask. I will show you how. I call you often beloved. Let me show the ways of the Master within. I will reveal all secrets when the illusion is surpassed into true reality.

And the particles that hold flesh together part and all thoughts become infinite: the particles those things that sustain you, form solid mass through the particles of thought projection moving; and then static, moving, then static. Particles that blow in the wind, not tied together in the illusion. What you see before you is a belief of solid. The solids are particles that blow in the wind. We are many forms through thought and particles we become those forms. In one breath we can disappear and become another form. We can play with color and light and sound and weave our magic. We are magicians, You and I beloved. Remember?

Part Three

Watching the stars at night I think of you. I gaze at the universe and galaxies and I wonder where you are and what you are doing and thinking. What is it that you need to achieve right now? And I look into my heart and I know all these answers and more. There are no more questions or unfinished stories. There is only our reunion. I long for your company in your wholeness and yet I have it here in my heart. You see beloved, all you're longing and yearning is mine and vice versa. Yet, when the time comes so close to completion, all that was: so challenging, disappointing, sad, heart wrenching, disappears in a moment. And, here we are in a new paradigm, a new way, a new future together.

I watched you once. You were sitting in a field, on the long grass, sketching the autumn day. And I watched you depict the beauty of nature and I whispered to you. "Not so far away are you from the real dream that beckons you forth. Meet me just half way and I will show you wonder beyond your imagination. Come dear one." But you felt me and did not hear. You were happy in that reality. And so, I stood back to rejoice in your happiness, and not interfere. You see my dear, I have waited eons for you to hear me again and celebrate our remembrance of one another. It was lying deep in your heart of hearts ready to awaken. And now of course you are that beautiful Princess that has awoken after a million years of sleep. Still we know we did what we had to do for it was our promise to God and ourselves to serve in any which way we chose. Yet the promise is fulfilled and thus now we are writing our story together before we move on to a place where our story does not matter; where we start again anew yet FREE to choose our destiny and creativity together. We could build new realms for those souls who need to reach contentment and peace. We could build castles and fjords if we so desire. We could build love clouds for angels to rest on. There are endless possibilities beloved. I await thee.

Part Four

So it is, my beautiful Princess. We still meet as Prince and Princess and we still flourish in each other's love. We are planning all the time for new adventures and how to exquisitely relate to the physical body to relinquish its hold on thee whilst not disappearing completely from the human realms. It is a delicate pursuit we follow indeed. Sometimes I see you rock with fear and trepidation yet the next day I see you fully resurface understanding that fears lying in our deepest crevice must be revealed and released. We are indeed, fighting in a comfortable way, for our right to be FREE. Every inch is another inch closer to our departure from the ways that we once knew. It is all as exciting as we acknowledge our strength and weaknesses yet know that our soul is ALL and especially together. And so it is.

Deliberately the mind is veiled from so much that goes on in the background. Twin Flames and other guides are working diligently to allow more information to come to the surface of those who are ready to take the leap of faith into ascension and movements towards channeling their own guidance. It is painstakingly designed to so to allow those guides on this side to interweave with those on the human side speaks; heightening your frequency as we lower ours. We meet somewhere in the middle through a very fine filter of consciousness attuned to a certain wave pattern. To catch this wave, your mind needs to learn to be still and alert. Fine-tuning is taking place for many now even those who are seemingly asleep are impressed to re-tune their instrument.

Part Five

As we await our true position and a lengthy process it must seem to you, we are realigning our aspects to one another in the higher realms. Each one is seen as a renewed marriage as to practice true consistency of energy and alignment. Even though you are not sure which aspects are aligned and which are not, I am making sure they are all aligned. You are already feeling that these aspects are within you now. And that is so. There will be a feeling of no separation and that is when you know the job is done. You have perceived for a long time the coming and going of my presence. Now you will perceive me as not separate. It is true to say that as a human in your era on earth, the trappings of the consumer world are enticing and the needs of the flesh need to be met in terms of food, clothes and shelter. Yet these activities are a lesser form of the need of your spirit and soul. The soul needs clothes in the form of rays of colors. It needs food in the form of Love. And it needs shelter in the realms of heaven. Choosing the beauty of the world to surround you is indeed a reflection of your souls needs. For the color of nature will feed you, Mother Earth Love will nurture you, and the sun will nourish you. Living as intended on Gods earth will bring you to a place of harmony within. More and more you as a society are turning to the simple pleasures of life. For the concrete surrounds and hustle bustle of city life cannot ultimately grant you your needs or your comfort. Rejoice each morn with the song of the bird, and retire with the whisper of my Love.

Part Six

As from my view and perception, that which you consider human frailty is fear based and not in your DNA but in your subconscious. This is easier to clear. Your DNA is perfected now. All you have to do is waiting for more of your talents, and light body comes to the fore. This may take weeks or months. I know you are patient beloved. And your patience has paid off.

The final layers are being peeled away to share your shiny divine self to the world permanently un-grazed by the human experience. You will be a shining example of how to ascend and you already are. We are now resting in the final branches of perfection. As you well know when the time is right you will be shown the next stage of flowering with all your petals awakened and blossoming. You're entire being freed from negative memory and false limitations and beliefs. All that is needed from you is to allow and go with the flow of expansion that is occurring for you and through you. We will walk all dimensions hand in hand offering pellets of wisdom and knowledge to those who wish to receive. Worry not dear one, they indeed will come.

TWIN FLAMES- Some Clarifications:

The level of integration with your soul spirit; that you have merged inside your own spiritual, emotional, mental, and physical bodies, always dictates what you get in a relationship mirror. What is important is what you're trying to heal in the self! All relationships mirror off this!

Basic definitions:

Your spiritual twin is usually, not in a body. This TWIN is your composite other half, when you were a pure ball of light, or creator; before you split into, or was born from the mother/father creations! This merge begins, only when, you're ready for the memory of living in an enlightened body or from the heart of the soul and spirit. This is an unconditional cellular love frequency or higher. This baseline, ultraviolet frequency spiking in your brain, is a must in order to initiate the original spirit blueprints to access your master spirit gifts. In numbers, this means a minimum level of four on a scale of seven.

Soul- twin or soul- task companions can come from a male soul group or female soul group that you merged with prior to earth, that you meet in this life, to help the soul group progress. These contacts happen, when you're integrating parallel lives/parallel soul aspects to infuse the soul in the body, in order to overcome death in the cells! This process, in progression, is called: soul infusion, resurrection, I AM enlightened body, or the crystalline, or the diamond ascension master body. In all cases, the soul and spirit is infused into the human cell form.

Task companions agree to clear old patterns and then have a choice to move on to merge another soul or spirit aspect. They could be considered archetypical energies, such as: warrior, priestess, or fool; not necessarily direct souls we have known! These archetypical wound patterns reflect the issues around soul agreements to clear the DNA in the family of origin, the soul family, or the creation family.

How do I know what my soul spirit purpose is?

ARTICLE- <u>Your Spiritual Brain- Interpreting Your Own Information</u>
You are all being called to live from a higher standard now, as you leave the old Earth behind. You are using the inner technology of healing. You are being asked to interpret the information and events (politics, religion, science, economics) you see and feel, as well as your own experiences from your soul purpose; not from your fears. This places you as your own sovereign authority; with your own new solutions, new adventures and creations of your own design, rather than repeating past lessons and wasting your energy in the in old Earth-dinosaur matrixes of death, disease, and suffering. As soul-infused humans with the immortal gene, you are helping Earth to re-create all her systems, so the greatest good of all humanity is served. Your inner Information, genius, and resources must be distributed across the planet at light/love speed. The old regimes will end up in service to the greater good of all or cease to be, as they follow your awakening.

<u>This is exactly what you're DNA blueprints were designed to do</u>, keep you opening up more and more information that is available just when you need it most! This allows the old Earth peoples to finish their lessons and their healing, while you create the new Earth. This state of being keeps you harmless, compassionate, and loving.

Now, if there remains a fragment emotion or belief, in most cases, it will no longer be about you because it belongs to the collective experience; but it can serve as a catalyst to push you to get the information you need to complete a task, solve a problem, or see the truth in an intimate exchange. This allows your own DNA to be in communication with you at all times! You must choose to live in separation or union with all other peoples and life forms. Can you simply let your DNA spiral of love; excite the DNA of another, to remember love or healing?

<u>Example:</u> What do you do when your partner, best friend, or child disagrees with you? Do you argue over a belief, who's the boss, or try to control the person or situation? Or, can you set a soulful boundary by saying:

- I can live my truth and still love you and be loved by you.
- I can live in my truth and not be hurt/abused by you or hurt/abuse you.
- When I express myself and live in my own love, I set a boundary so that all can make the highest choices for all concerned.

When we live in our own love, we live in our own channel. When we get our own special and **unique information**, we then live from the inside out; where events can no longer control us. Our individual brain information systems must become completely sovereign. The 10% Spiritual brain will be making a strong and unique call next. These spirit blueprints are the ones you brought from home when you were a creator. You simply add this blueprint information, to all that you have learned evolving in the human drama as a soul, and this blended information offers multiple choices/possibilities to experience and share with humanity. One must never know more about you than you know about yourself.

Politics, religion, philosophies, and even science will remain, only as constantly changing tools, to find solutions in our quickening evolution. But remember, your soul spirit's greatest gift is the free will to choose from the quantum field of information for any answer or need. Here true power, true choice, true genius, and equal love works for the good of all humanity, and any reality can be changed at any time!

Are you living in your own channel? Are you listening to your own information? Is every thought or feeling communicating with every cell and organ? If so, when you're so engaged with your own life and your own passion/focus, your love magnet sends the information through the quantum field to find all those who wish to create what has not been before! You designed your own blueprints well before Earth.

Don't you think its time to check your power meter and let these neural bio- nanites speak to you on your cell phone? You have your own internal nana-bio technology, molecular re-fabrication blueprints, your own bio-diesel fuel, and even a cosmic fuel cell within. Quite naturally your outer technology is evolving and models from your inner soul technology. The soul and the spirit have the original blueprints for that technology, which are stored within the human brain. The soul power in the body measures at 1.4 quadrillion horsepower, as it moves through the body's endocrine system to maintain perfect health. So, you are all free energy already! Isn't that the true nature of the power of love?

The technology of the old Earth regime: The old dinosaur's controlling genome projects, and base ET space devices from renegade secret agendas, will pale in comparison to the free energy power and genius of enlightened soul spirits manifesting from the awakened power of love technology. Just look around you and feel the quiet revolution in every corner of your planet, crying for change, freedom, and healthy commerce. And, what your collective still chooses to ignore, will continue to be acted upon you by your children, until you all listen/see from your God ears and eyes.

Many of you are just now living what you created five to seven years ago, showing you the intent and focus you used to manifest from playing with your future selves or potentials! Can you imagine living in your future all the time? These grander dejavu` moments will appear to be instant as we collapse the future and past into your exciting now! Be most proud that you have resurrected enough of your souls' from your wounded past to bring in a healed future!

How will I integrate all my soul spirit aspects in my body?

ARTICLE- *birthing your creator or spirit body*
Many of you are wondering "why", if you have completed the soul rebirthing, you're still recycling some negative emotions, and not yet into your new career or work. We hear you say, 'I thought I was done with that!" The simple answer is that the next step is re-mapping the spirit body in the DNA. That means both negative thoughts and feelings may arise around the creator families, rather than the soul families.

Leaving your parent families was joyful at first, as you created in polarity. Later judgments, shame, doubts, abuse, misperceptions and arguments around the experiment: dark/light, male/female, free will/control shattered many spirit families. Those remnant memories must now be resolved in your emotions and in your physical bodies, so that their negative effects are removed from this planet forever. Thus, the reminder, that when you're deleting old wounded parallel selves or existences that are or have been you; that you allow for brief stages of human and soul grieving. This includes: denial, anger, pain, blame, shame, doubt, rebellion, hurt, judgment, regret, addictive responses, depression, acceptance, and allowance. In this way you are sure that you are not running emotional addictions, but operating with detached compassion, as you access new downloads of information that must be integrated into the brain and throughout the body's endocrine system. These emotions recycle at the soul level, as well a when birthing the spirit, until the addictive response of the emotions are deleted from the brain and DNA synapses.

Parallel selves are positive or negative soul fragments of thoughts or feelings not owned from other existences that have been, or are still you, now.

Example: There could have been, a you, that lost all your wealth in the 1929 stock market crash, resulting in the loss of your family over this focus on money. In your present, it causes a continual paralyzing feeling of unworthiness.

A trade must be made to splice the DNA. The positive gift, the ability to manifest abundance must be exchanged for the wound of greed, at the expense of losses in love with family, so the body no longer re-creates or draws a similar experience. This way, the parallel self is not acting unconsciously and sabotaging the present moment!

When you heal a parallel self in the present moment, it doesn't exist on this planet or any other of your lifetimes. It doesn't exist on any other, planet, solar system, in any other creation or universe, and not in anyone else's life you've known in the past, present, or the future. It then also does not exist in your twin soul self or your twin spirit self, and has been integrated in your human body DNA, as the wisdom and gifts can be brought into this life to be used as a part of your genius. Now there is more room for a future self-potential. There is also room for powerful emotion, without being wounded by it.

Parallel selves merge and interchange in holographic realities, with the understanding that, you are all each other, and at some level have been each other, since we cross all experiences and have created together in our soul and spirit families, in time lines of past, present, or future. Indeed parallel perceptions collide into points of view, creating many universes and many Earths to play in.

Future selves, allow you to activate a potential self, the moment you sit in your heart chamber and image what you desire to create next. You are then in optional moments of: conscious healing which is body regeneration/ cell replication; the moment of conscious creation which is precipitation; the moment of conscious body orgasm/ bliss which is self love; the moment of self reflection or harmless world compassion; and the moment of conscious travel which is teleportation.

Such, are some natural gifts of your soul body and your spirit body, when the clear blueprints are re-spliced in the body's stem cells.

Now include the multitudes of unique genius that each of you brought with you to help heal Earth as well as the entire universe on your return back to your newly formed soul groups and creations. Many of you are already beginning to communicate with, and exchange new information with these groups, so that you will finally get to live in a warm satisfying feeling of love!

SELF MANTRAS for BIRTHING the SPIRIT BODY:

- Spirit, if I leave my body, make sure you are in it with me, so when we return in just a few Earth minutes from our adventures in no time.
- Spirit, I understand true body power as balance and sharing myself with others.
- Spirit, I feel true power when I listen & act & Source my desires from you, rather than, the needs of my lower self: survival, fear, control, or unworthy.
- Spirit, you make me worthy to stay in my body & have all I so desire!
- Spirit, put me on your automatic pilot.
- Spirit, my twin soul and my twin spirit are one!
- When I focus on the blend of the male/female as one, I channel my Higher Self.
- Spirit, merge in my body and take me out of time!
- All my cells and nerves are now conscious in love.
- My throat will never feel my twin, split in judgment ever again!

How do I know if I'm channeling my higher self?

ARTICLE - *Channeling Your Own Higher Self*
It is a long story for many, and I know saying it is risky, but I must, because it is such a part of the old Earth energy. The story tells us that it is time to channel our own Holy Self and trust your own inner information from your own heart's gut and body sensate.

There are people, dear misguided souls that climb into our channels and channel our own master information back to us; and we think it is there channeling, when they are simply using our channel to channel us back to us! That is acceptable when another is being asked to help us channel our own Holy Spirit to reclaim our records or heal our body's DNA blueprints.

But, it can also be dangerous when or if they steal the life force energy from us, as we put them on a pedestal, and give them all our love, **NOT KNOWING THAT IS OUR** own **GOD LOVE WE ARE FEELING** and **NOT THEIRS**!

This happens because they don't love themselves; though they fear being alone and powerless, and they are so angry at God; they appear loving, but under it is a desperation and control to ride on some light that will give them purpose and meaning because somewhere, somehow, long ago they destroyed their own light; and yes, it is all just a story they believe is real! But when they are desperate they will travel about, crying out to be saved and it is very subtle, very subtle; and you wake up in the night and they are crawling in your bed and body! They want your life, you, and everything; so very subtle, so very subtle. The drain is not noticed till you try to leave and do your own thing, then comes the sting! You become so confused, you begin to feel their desperation, pain; their death and utter hopelessness; their merge into your being; and then you feel things God never intended that you should have to experience! In bewildered exhaustion, you wonder what happened to love and begin to wonder who you are!

Read this story well, though it may shock you, there is many a great master healer who did not heed this instruction and it devastated their life or caused death to the body, if they did not see it in time! THAT IS NOT LOVE. It is enmeshment and 'bottom feeding' of the most insidious kind. The sad part is, that often the one who is doing it, is the most dangerous because they are not in charge of self and they do not realize they are the culprit!

Have you healed your deep/ultimate fear of being rejected, or just replaced it with mystical addictive allusions of being worshipped and loved by others in ego service?

Remember, once you have sealed the connection to your higher self, then your safely connected to the universal telephone lines throughout the universe. No one can speak you without the "per-mission" of your own soul spirit and in the alignment of its agenda. This gives you comfortable access to any information: guide, master, angle, soul group, world federation, or council, you might need to fulfill your life path.

Test it for yourself. Observe whose` life your living and what price is being asked under the disguise of what? Only you can answer those questions. Observe, observe, and stay awake to yourself and you will know! Ask yourself, "does this self love"? **If you're going to offer true service to humanity it must be in integrity for the greatest good of all concerned and without judgments or hidden agendas attached.**

Check the inner wounded healer list below to evaluate yourself to see what you are offering/ attracting:

- Does the information I'm receiving make sense? Does it smack of control, fear, manipulation, or not come from unconditional love? Am I one with my Higher Self or channeling my lower self?
- Do I try to channel for everyone else, or do I simply hold the love in reflection, so they can channel from their own soul spirit, asking me to assist where I am needed?
- **Can my love excite their DNA to spiral with mine?**
- Are you talking with or at the person or group and really allowing them in?\

- Have you healed your deep, ultimate fear of being rejected, or just replaced it with mystical addictive allusions of being worshipped and loved by others in ego service?
- Are you helping people come to a choice or telling them what to do?
- Are you putting service above self love, or can you just change the world by changing you!
- Is your service sharing your love and experience, or unconsciously insisting others believe as you do?
- Am I forcing my love or dreams on others, making me a spiritual bully?
- Do I use truth as a weapon?
- Am I trying to help people who don't need my help, or am I just a wounded healer?
- Am I able to hold positive emotions equal access as the negative addictive ones: of loss, rejection, self hatred so I don't self implodes in my addiction to negativity?
- Do I do service with a hidden agenda, living off another's light; to feed off another person, place, circumstance, or event? Can I live on my own light and just share?
- Am I still working to prove or compete for my worth?
- Can I just heal others by being in my Self and by watching them heal themselves within my own PRESENCE?
- Am I open/honest/ true (REAL) or do I use manipulation, denial, or control to get what I want?
- Do I trust my Holy Spirit as my Source and provider first, or am I looking for or addicted to, the search for an outer twin soul or twin flame to save me.
- AM I aware of how I unconsciously invade other people's energy for advantage?

- AM I carrying any of these un-answered soul questions in my body or energy field?

How do I know what my level of channeling is?

ARTICLE: *Levels of Channeling for Your Discernment:*
By Azraelus- contact Jayne Chilkes: for classes or sessions
http://theangelschannel.netfirms.com

Stage One
Base Ego - Kindergarten levels up to about stage three
Signs: Early psychic awareness, cards, psychometrics etc. utilizing solar plexus, lower ego self, base astral, self opinionated messages, dogmatic, subconscious interference, conditional.Not healing

Stage Two
Ego/Conditional
Some basic mediumistic skills, awareness of spirit guides e.g. American Indian, Chinese man, etc, ego self of guides, base astral, self opinionated messages, drawn to be a healer, subconscious interference.

Stage Three
Ego/Conditional and Unconditional
Complete awareness of spirit guides, working as a medium, trance medium, spiritual church activities, proof of life after death, family members passed over, clearing some past lives, intermediate ego self, self opinionated messages, subconscious interference, becoming a healer.

Stage Four
Ego/ Higher Self/ Loving
Intermediate Level
Awareness of higher vibrations of angels, masters etc, clearing past levels, messages from masters, spirit guides and merging guides with masters, false masters, inconsistent messages, mundane psychics, some lower ego self, intermediate ego self, higher ego self, some higher self, some soul work, still

dealing with stage one to three at times, unconditional love growing stronger, full strong healer, becoming fully self aware to clear all blocks, self honesty medium to high.

Stage Five

Divine Love/Finely Tuned Subconscious/ Higher Self/Clarity

Pure Soul, Divine Love, Soul Family/Group Awareness, consistent flow, ascension work, spiritual psychology, wisdom, residue of past life, this life work, masters, angels, twin flame reunion, Christ-ed self, god self awareness, higher self, purity, purification stages one to four and use in some way, little future or mundane messages, healer of all levels of being, little interference of subconscious if any.

Stage Six

Mastered

Choice to channel or not, twin flame unified, Christ-ed self – apparent; full ascension.

How can I be sure that my past will no longer haunt me?

ARTICLE - *SPIRIT LIVING-POLISHING THE REAL SELF –Straight talk*
Are you still suffering from the hesitation of spiritual whining or arrogance; complain, complain! You chose to be you on this path; on earth at this time, and you are not a victim of it! "How", you ask? Keep it simple. Just let being you be a discovery. Whatever you focus on-you create! Where is your focus? A negative focus causes the peptides in the receptor sites to addict to emotional over reactions. Where is your focused creating? Where is your focused imagination, because that is exactly what you will receive? Is you're on the old stories and the old games or is it on a playfully creative solution?

Let it be the first day of your life! Let go of the old story and the old games, as they are just another escape, no longer able to protect you from death; just keeping you from being in the moment of accepting whatever comes to more deeply engage you, inside yourself.

What about just being you, not broken, flawed or walked in/out of, soul braided, soul merged, or any other identity; but just exploring life, just exploring you. Isn't that what matters and isn't that why you're here? Can you forget the old stories, old games, and old identities and let this be the first day of your life? Only living life can protect you from death. Does everything need an ontological, cosmological explanation, or is that just another old game, another escape! Can you finally unfetter from your limitations?

Soon the cosmic connection to other realities will be normal here, so do you don't want to miss out on your own life. Can you say yes to life: no more hiding, no more judging the human experience, and understanding that no one has done anything wrong to you or you to another; that you all wanted all possible experience?

Can you just be being willing to be you? You are not lost and you know why you're here. There is nothing left to channel except yourself and when you don't know what that is, let the moment guide you; simply be in the moment of love, whatever that offers you!

The Tao or the Way, has never been put down in words, rather it is left for the seeker to discover within!

God, The All In All, is love and we are all that love, just here playing, while none of us are who we say or think we are. It is time to forget the old human stories and games that blame God, which is just another game! You're not broken and you don't need fixing and all your aspects alive inside you, when you decide they are. Let your voice be the one voice of freedom's; the freedom from all human mistakes. You're in charge and the old game was fun but there is more waiting if you decide to be you! They, those beyond the veils, are waiting for you, while you think your waiting for them! You're the anchor for them. You're the doer here. The archangels just send light rays of love! There is no longer a "they," because it's whatever you do that matters to you and gets matched in he outer world, by those in other realities that you represent. That is the only "they" you need. Is it dead man sleep walking, or god man/woman self realized walking?

In your blind spots, your own prison, you are simply assigning power outside; another escape from your choices! You're already more evolved than any other lifetime. Next life, please call for new experience, a new story. You've never taken charge before and its now just a decision; it's an attitude that you're saying it like you mean it for the first time, so its time to write new records and burn the old ones! Either you're a God or your not? Which is it? That's what you have to answer to the "theys" or the "thems". So, you're running out of the old friends, the old habits, the old addicts. The new Earth will have none of it! There is nothing left to do but open, trust, stay in the moment, ask for what you need, take charge of your life through focused choices and be yourself. You do know who that is, every time you do something for self; every time you focus on self, then all those multiple voices will become one!

No more gaming, no past stories, no core patterns, not one self judgment; just you, just now. Are you love or not? It is simple; then all of matter will rush to your avail. Decide dear sweet creation; decide unless you're a fence sitter, addicted to an old story like a sleep walking human. But you know better and that makes you culpable. You create your reality absolutely, without exception no matter who you might think you are here, and that applies to all levels! There is no violation in any reality! Your circuits just need you to connect naturally, never mind the rest! What matter asks, is for movement into your own life, taking care of self, and deciding to show up for life. Your body and emotions will follow. Those old voices will attempt to give you an identity till you decide you're committed to life and then they will unify in your own voice, without bottom feeding off the dramas.

Any unfinished unresolved feelings will show up on your daily plate in a way you can handle and offers largeness to life. Life cannot be controlled it must be lived in your own biological bonding and time sensitive encodings, as all time lives within you now! Imagine living without one single limitation and not missing out on your own life. Value your privacy as well, because it is also part of your most intimate moments with the world! Let the world and others have their own experience of themselves. Your experience is yours alone. You may no longer need to be special, just unique, as you see yourself again as part of the ONE love. Then, no longer will you be hurt by life or will you hurt with it. You know that evolution and creation did/does work, because you helped create it! So, what did you discover new about yourself today?

And so I repeat, any judgment on life claims an answer! The angel in you must embody and choose life to end the fear that it's your fault that physical reality doesn't work well and is screwed up; that humans are fodder, and creator goofed!

Can you engage in your life and focus on what matters; take care of self: cook, roll in the mud, write a book, make an art of living life, create, play outside, live life for yourself, and stop hurting yourself with life, so you will stop hurting?

Can you stay in your own reality so you won't have to control other's love? Can you accept dominion over what you choose to feel? Can you enjoy the simple things: the natural five senses of taste, touch, smell, hearing and feeling; the Earth/air/fire/water that have always kept you alive after a dark night with other humans, or your soul!

In Effect: There was no war in heaven, no angelic rebellion, no intergalactic wars; no separation. That's mankind's story on God. Third density reality is an illusion made of matter, for learning and experience. God does not do what humans do. God is Love, joy, playfulness, creating, and all those wonderful attributes are stored in your DNA, once you give up your old Earth human drama stories you created. Do not assign your human attributes to God; only when they are to resolve the soul's agenda to master polarity for wisdom, will you enjoy your future lives. Is it possible, to eventually return to what you already are, and that is love dear ones?

Journal your own mantras

- I choose to engage in my own life!
- I have no past and live in the present moment.
- I discover new things about myself each day
- I accept the human experience as a part of all life.
- I replace those old voices with my own holy-spirit directives.
- I no longer need to special or different, as I recognize we are all part of the one!

As **Sa**

Twin Flame Counterparts

Merge | Separation **Duality** **Matter | Spirit**

Angel — Angelica

Open Heart — Your Angel Self

What happens to my old earth body once I have rebirthed or ressurected my soul?

ARTICLE - *The Old Earth Body Says Goodbye!*
Our old earth bodies with their emotions and old beliefs have finally surrendered. They are giving up all the excuses as to why our little inner-child can't be loved. Do you not feel that everyone and everything is dropping out of your body? As the old programs leave the body, there is apathy, an emptying, and a depression. The body gives up all the battles and surrenders into acceptance. There is no energy to return to the old life, as the new energy is being stored or, rewired in the brain, the new purpose and passion awakens to action. For the first time in any life true choice, true free will visits and asks to stay!
It is quite normal after **the dark night of the soul is purged**, for the body to grieve all its old lives of limitation, suffering, loss, and wiriness of every birth and death. Now there is room for the soul to safely live in the body without the enslavement, limitation, and abuse. Once these negative feelings leave the body and the polarity stops struggling, then the soul smiles in the body and begins to Live, allow, accept life and love the self in freedom, for what seems like the first time in any lifetime.

The old earth body must be dropped so the new earth body can live without the fear of disease, death, or poverty. So, what is necessary where you can and allow the body to speak to you and tell you how to nurture it, until, quite naturally the soul takes over. But old habits are the last temptation of being human, and the anger at accepting the human experience.

The old body asks many questions: "Why did I come to Earth, why did I agree to mix a compassionate DNA with one of power; the mother/father lovers, our human and spirit parents/selves? They don't seem to mix. I'm angry with myself and Source, for buying into an experiment, which has seemingly turned into enslavement. I'm angry at Source for the choices I made. I'm angry from splitting off from my Twin Flame; I'm angry at myself for not creating what I wanted, for so long."

Our anger has masked our fear and now we are down to the Divine anger in the cells and we are asked by the body to give up trying to control what has hurt us. No one can hurt one who is self-loving. This is just the body ego that is dying! The body tries to distract us in to our old addictions to maintain control, but even that is just the body crying out for sacred touch and love!

The ego body clings to the past with a false sense of thinking that it can control the soul! That is the last laying down of the cross, the old life, the old self, the old fears, hatreds, and judgments; the last of letting the old human-self go! It will spit out illness, anger and desperation; anything to hang on until immortality is reborn in the forever.

We have walked out of our pasts and the "valley of humiliation," and taken our bodies to a place where the soul, and later the spirit, can totally indwell and live in freedom to bring through fully, our spiritual gifts on Earth. This was the promise made to us before we came to earth: It seems so hard to accept that we can have it. The new Earth begins and our bodies are coming with us! Indeed, we are tentative to accept a new passion and purpose with our own worth, and we are not sure what to create or who we fully are yet!! But it is naturally inside our individual DNA and is under the old Earth body! That is why the energies are so physical. There is no "Grace time" to hide. We must be honest with ourselves and ask for what we want, knowing, and be ourselves along side others, while we share our gifts with the world.

We must accept our fear and anger without making them orphans, love what we have been, and somehow trust that it is easier to go forward, than stay with the old friends of fear, abuse, and powerlessness. We must invoke the new nerve system that is in the brain to be active in the soul of the heat and in the body. New ideas, people, divine actions and energies will come forth quite naturally. This is the new soul's neural system, ready to trigger action in Love!

Our must be organic now.

Are we lighter-hearted peoples now? Will we now re-enter life and accept every challenge as a joy of being alive, and able to participate in life, knowing that the eyes of our neighbor may be their last glance in this life? Do we see the God in everyone and everything? Can we arise as if it is the first day of our life? Can we bring our deepest desires into attraction and execute them into our hands and use? This is natural pleasure coming from a natural imagination. Human angels are able to blend spirit and matter through the organic feeling of joy! Soul-infused humans and spirit-infused humans love to express their purpose! That is what evolution on Earth offers them.

No **synthetic substance or addictive emotion** can replace or keep away such splendor! The heart initiates the natural pleasures of joy! All our other selves, our soul spirit, all realms and dimensions live within us now. We are everything and everything is us! Such Oneness simplifies life and allows us to merge and synchronize our technologies with our true feelings. The danger, as always, is that we will revisit pleasure or use false feelings to distance ourselves from intimate connections with ourselves, or others.

We will create, from the inside out, of these very bodies. If we continue to live in the past, it will consume us once again. If we choose to live in our organic state of creativity, which is the same as our soul purpose and service to humanity, then every moment will be a birthing! Can our technological toys and tools be, but after-thoughts of the heart? Will we imagine, in through our breath, sharing our love with life and watch while simple magic arrives at our doors? Will the simplicity of divine action also execute or magnetize our joys to those we want to play with? What will you choose in your next life Earth cycle?

Check your "Today I," New Life Quotient in the Life Commitments below!

It will give you an overall attitude index of your old/new Earth attitudes

- TODAY I see the god in everyone and everything and I Love what I see. I choose to accept my power. I choose to be happy. Today is the best day of my life! Today I will learn something new. Today I live in the present.

- TODAY I will change a limited belief! I am happy with my decisions. I AM lighter. I will give love and understanding to all the people in my life! I will listen to life. I see the perfection in every one and everything! I have clarity and understand all things now!

- TODAY I am light hearted and no longer carry the world's problems on my shoulders. I receive unconditionally as I experience greater abundance and supply! I forgive myself for my ignorance. I have the opportunity for a joyful adventure. I always experience miracles. Today I AM in peace.
- TODAY I acknowledge that I AM GOD also. I have unconditional genius, wealth, and immortality (ageless) and always have. I AM aware of my choices. I AM fully awakened. Today I arise, grow, and greet the beautiful day! I can do anything I want and enjoy my life.
- TODAY I am the unconditional receiver of radiant health, radiating light, and timelessness! I have plenty of time.
- TODAY I remember who I AM and I KNOW why I AM here! I AM protected and have courage! I AM the master of time.
- TODAY I AM the Master of energy. I AM a powerful manifesting God. I AM awakened. I AM greater than my body! I AM fulfilled and protected. I AM worthy, fearless, fulfilled, unlimited.
- TODAY I AM psychic, enlightened and imaginative. I Am ONE with ALL Life. I AM all knowing. I AM precipitating gold in my veins. I Am a genius, talented, and a healer in the now! I AM joyful, free, and radiant. I can teleport, walk through walls, change matter. I am precognitive. I Am love expressing. I AM in the union of my Holy Spirit.

How do we emerge in our new muti-dimensional cell body?

ARTICLE - *Regaining Your Angel Wings for Your Next Channeling System*

Your newly blended cell body is coming on line in the brain, heart, and sacral cradle neural pathways to receive new information. Many are experiencing the stray remnant memories from the primal reflexes in the psychological pain body. If you're experiencing any of these effects, simply breathe through the whole body: a color, a symbol, and a sound. The electro-magnetic bubble or spiral around your body will rotate counterclockwise to empty out ancient negative cell programs or daily accumulations. Your spiral can then rotate clockwise, ready to manifest from loving, colorful, sounds, and symbols. Aren't these called your **angel wings?**

Example: Use your body as a tuning fork, an I-pod, or a cell phone. Remember that heart sounds, colors, and symbols, can now substitute for: instant creating, receiving or sending information, and any/ all forms of healing, as they are a higher frequency than words and language. This can simplify and refine your spiritual practice in minutes and bring you into the next form of channeling, thereby avoiding over processing the limitation of a limitation. The harmless cells have conscious permission to release, so the body can never again act off of fear or any form of judgment.

Your cellular soul phone makes calls from your own heart as you send healing or love on another's behalf. Never underestimate the power of sharing these colors, sounds, and symbols that you witness/ request for another or the planet. Today, sharing one symbol message of: healing, creation, or invention, can offer dramatic changing choices and outcomes for your world and all your parallel selves that live throughout the universe. Imagine and breathe a pearl fuchsia with An AH-OOH sound in the heart, to stop inner conflict and empower yourself above the thoughts of the mass consciousness. A red-orange sun symbol desalinates water for alchemical cell restructuring. Opalescent silver purifies all cells and allows trust to re-bond into cellular love.

Other colors: Turquoise- brain capacity and telepathic communication; royal blue- adjusting the magma of the earth and the human spine alignment; pearl green- highest outcomes individual or soul purpose in groups; pearl salmon- right and self loving choices; Opalescent Emerald- purifies inner/other pollution; Diamond light- Peaceful co-existence with all life. Peach- absolute love manifests directly from your Spirit's will. Feel free to use those sounds, symbols, and colors that are unique to your own protocols and situations.

Check your **cell index,** to see what your spiral needs to empty or fill with, accelerating your DNA through your **light field.** Allow it to feel flexible, fluid, and spontaneous. This allows the lower and your upper Merkaba triangles to blend and spin your inter-dimensional Love spiral of life, or your bliss/enlightened body.

Counter spiral rotation- Empty your closed heart cell index:

- Constant internal arguing of the lower and higher selves, with an inability to integrate the twin flame body, and parallel bodies.
- Trauma based survival mechanisms resulting in the body fighting against itself, where the endocrine system pumps emotional addiction, physical death, and reality perversions that replace natural emotions.
- Rage at the Higher Self separation: for not protecting you as an infant in the womb, from abuse that resulted in: fragmented, shattered, ego identity structures with disassociated thoughts and feelings, that put you in constant identity crisis and a hopeless sense of the loss of self.
- Stripping the self regulating control of the child's neural- biological bonding responses that allow him to bond his cells in regenerative love, within a sense of self, while stimulating organic emotions.
- Self hatred in a defensive shock mode that no longer trusts self, humans, or life. A constant wounded inner dialogue nags: "Love

hurts; this is too much pain to bear; Life disappointments me; I'll never be happy; I feel lost and don't know who I am; I can't handle darkness; I don't feel connected; I'll never find my soul's purpose; I'll die if I open my heart!"

- Relationship controls entail arguments over: sexual body attitudes, identity definitions of self, changes in consciousness states, life purpose and direction, intimacy needs, and manifesting mutual creative solutions.
- Prolonged enslavement: religious or sexual cult survivors, war survivors, domestic battering, as the re-enactment of ancient ancestral, unspeakable practices, unnatural acts.

Clockwise spiral rotation- Fill your Inner guided cell index with:

- A strong sense of self identity, focused passionate creativity, playful self satisfaction, flexible and interdependent relationships, inner connection to the oneness of all life, confidence, soul-spirit directed, self sustaining, resilient, and adaptive, imagination is the workshop.
- Their inner dialogue says, 'I know that: I can find the answer I need; that there is someone/ ones that I can share my love with; the Earth is awakening and I can serve with my gifts; everyone is on their spiritual path-no matter the appearances. Earth is a challenging school and all humanity is healing together; I am excited to be a part of our new multi-universe as it evolves through Earth; Feel me as I feel you, or I am my holy spirit!

As the planet quickens its awakening, relevant but simple, energy tools help keep our light fields clean, clear, and update our neural DNA, to make quick decisions in service, that are one with your joy! Did you spin your Love field today? Over the course of the next 200 years, all our DNA/RNA strands will be blended into a new race called Peace, where all spirals are flowing in/out each other in multitudes of creative, yet experiential love!

How will we our bodies travel and out of time on the new Earth

ARTICLE - *Understanding Time AND Time Travel Holograms:*
When we are in a state of unconditional love, or ultraviolet frequency in the brain, we collapse time. In this state of "now," we are able to heal the past and bring in future potentials. By deleting or turning off old circuits in the brain, we make way for new ones to be connected. This is one of the most efficient tools we have for creating!

Yet, we pay little attention of our ability to alter time, through an intense passionate focus, on what we want to create, to the exclusion of any intrusive thought. Unconditional love is the tool that allows us to change anything or ourselves in an instant.

When this focus is mastered fully, the heart focus connects the lower and upper body into an energetic spiral that traverses the speed of light or love. This spiral can propel, when cycling fast enough, the body to bi-locate, fly, remote view, soul travel, or create miracles. This quantum spiral acts directly off the dormant, virgin, or super-conscious strands within our DNA to know anything from the data-base in the brain and be responded to from a universal library of information.

We inhabit a "multi-dimensional universe" in which several dimensions of different vibration (al) states co-exist simultaneously. Higher dimensions move faster at and above the speed of light. Lower dimensions move slowly until they occupy matter states. Because of this, the soul can operate many bodies of experience at the same time (parallel lives).

Holograms are simply known or unknown time or spatial reference points, thought forms, or brain images associated with people, places, times, events, or circumstances. These come from interrupted light wave fields that contain all life information as a library: This is like having a movie playing in your head. A desire, a thought, a feeling, or an attitude searches for knowing to validate itself as a truth. So, past and future selves are parallel reflections of self while still in a human body, through personal or collective genetic memory. So what fears or limitations, you resolve in the NOW, you automatically resolve in the past, present, and future!

Remote Viewing

Remote viewing is the use of mental and/or emotional imaging outside the present moment of time to observe past or future events. Governments often use remote viewing technique to observe circumstances, events or places of other countries for security purposes. In this scenario, human consciousness operates like technology.

Soul travel

Soul travel allows one to travel or focus their energy into another frequency of experience, while still fully conscious in the body. As one understands the lessons or experience from another time, one begins to feel a shift of vibration in the form of sounds, colors, and electro-magnetic body pulses or; humming sensations in the human heart and brain that accompany the movement between time and space, where one is both the observer and participant of an experience. Other realities, time frames, or information are referenced for growth or change by using the pineal gland as an imaging video camera It is only a matter of time before the human body can bi-locate or teleport if the codes in an individual DNA can re-remember this natural ability.

The Quality of the Attribute DNA Strands allows us to collapse time:

It is time that allows us .to master the character attribute strands in the DNA. Most certainly your body has **genome sequences** for every, gland, organ, and function; but the most important, are the character attributes in the DNA sequencing, which are based on mastering experiences through an emotional base. This is the main channel to the soul spirit. It opens up access to the 90% of the brain that has been dormant due to the lack of use, or shall we say the trade off we all made; to play the game of free will evolution at the lowest human density possible! As we engage in lifetimes of experience in either soul bodies or spirit bodies, we re-gain and initiate memory in our DNA. The first step is to clear the past soul blueprint patterns.

Negative blueprints of learning from the past contain: suffering, hate, judgment, or other limited polarity emotions or thoughts. Once completed, the natural spirit blueprints that fire from thought forms of unconditional love are remembered automatically: independence, detachment, compassion, resourcefulness, determination, self-expression, genius and freedom.

However, to forever delete a neuron from a negative attribute, it takes 3 to 90 days to excite a new net in the brain sequencing, assuming that the personality doesn't disconnect it through an old addictive response. It only takes 17 seconds of pure focus for a new creation to be imprinted on the frontal lobe of the brain. For surely, a cancer cell in an unworthy spleen, an angry liver, abused mind, fearful kidneys, or a grieving heart, can't re-sequence its own DNA.

Many souls on Earth have spent many lifetimes trying to open their own original sequences by gaining wisdom from every possible thought or feeling offered in the human experience. In some cases, only a few lessons per lifetime were focused on. The power of the emotions cannot be underscored.

The spirit blueprint, when called on, can indeed give each organ and cell, a function; its perfect blueprint to self-replicate. You must initiate it by asking the DNA for it, which is a supreme act of self-love and belief, while being willing to accept that you will let go of the old negative thoughts, feelings, or beliefs that caused the cells to fight for life. Your body knows, quite naturally, how to heal itself. Your passion, imprinted on the pineal gland, allows the brain to call up the new program.

What's in your DNA? The human angel is the prize of all universes in its ability to feel, image, choose, and create in an Eternal body. You don't have to die to go into your next life: Simply raise the frequency of the body you're already in and you will feel differently. That feeling is what so many label as, another dimension.

Will we be telepathic on the new Earth?

ARTICLE - *Telepathy is mind to mind communication:*
We could also say it is God's Universal mind or thoughts in our human brain, and we know that the first thought, was love. Have you talked in your inner silent-mind voice to a relative on the other side lately; sat inside the imagination of a gossamer butterfly, or sent a beautiful message to your lover's heart who dialed your cell phone at that instant?

Much like a telephone, the human, the soul, and the spirit each have their wiring to the human brain. The connections or signals can be: electrical, radio, internet, wireless, or quantum. The very circuits in your brain have the same connections with an organic conscious base. Are you a God conscious organic computer encased in a Mother board of Love with the world as your Father board? Then, your lower cerebellum is the hard drive, your midbrain has the software, your frontal lobe, (emotion brain), is the laser imaging-device, and your heart-voice turns you on and off through your desired passions or focus. The brain signals through the spine to the main glands, who talk to organs, which speak to every cell, until a circular spiraling bubble of electro-magnetic waves flow back through the physical body to: the emotional body, to the mental body, and through the intuitive body and back to the mind of God, in the circle of life. At any moment, any human can contact its Source for whatever is desired in the Heart's mind.

The neo-cortex is the language area of the brain, which controls language for the purpose of communication and speech in human evolution. Some call this the yellow monkey brain, the "Towel of Babel," or the mind of the collective unconscious. Before we entered the human experience, did we all speak one language? Did we speak the language that angels made? Was it the language of light, color, and sound patterns of Love? Don't we still carry these code patterns in our DNA?

When a planetary soul species is ready to move into unconditional love, then the heart unites with the midbrain or super-conscious connections to the spiritual DNA blueprint. All talents, gifts, and abilities from the past, present, or future present multiple choices for whatever reality you desire to experience. Usually, the more experience embodies, the more wisdom to add to the original blueprint. Love is never wasted. We could call this a global, universal, or quantum brain and we could call our bodies crystalline love computers.

If you consider the history of Earth, there was a major epoch in Lemuria, prior to Atlantis in which most humans remember; when humans communicated with the plants, animals, each other, and their inter-dimensional origins without abuse, and lived in harmony. Many civilizations have come and gone from this planet with such genius abilities, so why can't we? Our DNA has cloned out those stem cell memories due to man's violence against himself and his creations. But, this ability to directly communicate with all life forms lies dormant within each of us, as we trust the natural awakening of our DNA back to self-love.

True telepathy is not the seduction of mind control, in sending and receiving messages that are contaminated with hidden agendas or secrecy. There are myriads of stories about black magicians, dark lords, and those who wanted to be masters of the universe using mass thought control within the DNA. Indeed, it has influenced this planet and the entire universal experience.

True receiving is based on the neutrality and harmlessness of unconditional love, where the message can be received and interpreted by the receiver in terms of their own integrity. It is the brain's decoder that searches for messages that want to share the same phone line or frequency. Pure, pristine, or virgin thought communication has a base frequency of a ultra-violet brain cycle.

When we send a message or thought of hatred, anger, hurt, or maligned negative thoughts to another through our mind, then we are limited to the telecommunications we can receive back. We also tie up our own brain circuits, as well as that person's brain so they cannot receive freer soul or human reception. There are only so many brain circuits open to receive messages at any given time!

These seemingly non-physical receivers affect the very quality of your daily experiences and communication in all relationships. What limited messages are you sending and receiving? Furthermore, when your soul spirit is trying to contact you, are all your telephone lines too busy to reach your imagination and give you the very answers that are in the library in your own mind? Can you dial a question to the universe on the gamma ray or cosmic ray frequency and find a new invention; or be shown an image of the place you lived before Earth? Why would you need a cell phone when you can send a message to the whole of the world with one thought? Just remember, negative thoughts travel slower and positive or loving thoughts travel at the speed of love/light or faster, shortening your desire made manifest. What's in your thoughts today? Does the thought of "not being enough," form a limited belief. If we add up all of our negative thought beliefs, then what does our telepathy say?

Finally, we must consider that if thoughts are composed of light patterns, then man can look in the mirror, bend light and see his own god reflection. This thought to see/know self opens the illusion of time, where a universal library of information reveals an imagination of multiple potentials. This is the moment of love, where man realizes that his free will allows him to remove from his very brain any limited experience of fear, hatred, or suffering, forever, and: The lessons in those thought-feeling forms have also been mastered forever. He then sends a new telepathic message out to all those in the human; in the soul, and in the dimensions of non-time that he is free: to create a new reality because his telepathy in his beautiful mind has been renewed. One telepathic thought has changed his very world and all those in the universe he lives with! So, as you think and believe, you get to experience and influence all life with, even to the slightest of moments! Allow yourself to notice the outcome of sending loving thoughts to a person, place, circumstance, or event. The person or event rises up to a more loving outcome. When we deposit loving thoughts into a person's Holy bubble, it is like putting money in their bank account and remains throughout all time, until they call upon it in a time of need or desire. Your thoughts and beliefs are what you feed yourself, and all others in the world. They are the messengers for creating your reality. Guard them as wise and precious gifts. Thought pollution brings war, death, suffering, and dramatic earth changes.

The planet is <u>one</u> telepathic web, where every thought counts, where just one thought can change the world and where the universe will answer. The evolution of earth is measured by all the negative and positive thoughts on any given day and these form-beliefs. I challenge you to let go of all your beliefs and empty your thoughts. What is your telepathic message now?

How do our brain waves process information from the soul spirit?

ARTICLE: - *Your Brain Connects You to the Universe Through Cycles.*

Brain Wave Cycles:
These waves in the brain determine the states of consciousness that we create from. One can think of cycles as images or flash-frames on a video screen. Whatever visual or auditory information you take in each hour dictates exactly what the brain will feed out to the world. If you watch TV/ virtual reality all day, then those are the reality images or experiences you will cycle into your life. If you empty the screen and use your imagination, then there are trillions of frames of images and new information to imprint from dormant, virgin DNA material. If you are trying to create in a theta state or meditation and you fall asleep, you are losing the major effect of the theta creation. It is best to create in the theta cycles so the neuron-nets can decode. The criteria for each cycle are listed below.

Application:
Using the Definitions below, Check to see what states you feed Your Brain with? How Much Time do you spend in the Theta Creative State?

Beta is the **waking state** when our brain waves operate from 14 to 40 cycles per second. This is a time when we are involved in basic insights, understanding daily activities, basic cognition, and knowing.

Alpha is a **dream state or waking dream REM state** when our brains operate from 7 to 14 cycles per second. It is a preliminary connection to the subconscious and subliminal connection with creativity. The focus is normal life problem solving and a place of affirmations, visualizations, and prayer.

Theta is a **meditative state** or place of consciously creating and imaging. It is a place where stress is reduced; higher creativity and choices are also accessed through midbrain and lower cerebellum activity. Activity operates from 4 to 7 cycles per second. Time collapses as past, present, and future become one. In Theta, quantum leaps are possible. Behaviors can be easily changed in states of intuition, ESP, remote viewing, and higher psychic brain connection; states of "magic," where past realities can be changed or new realities can be manifested. This is not a state to be highly emotionally reactive in, or bring problems to; else they get re-created and amplified! This is a state of pure creation!

Delta is a **sleep state or coma state** where deep healing and detached awareness exist. Here, the brain is operating at less than 4 cycles per second. Deep-body cellular regeneration and repair is accessed and is instrumental in overcoming death in the body. Perhaps this is the state where the "near death" experience is portrayed.

What will the Earth bodies begin to feel like?

ARTICLE - *Living in a Higher Frequency Body:*
Quantum Physics has proven that emotions condense as energy particles and if they are not expressed, they become lodged in spaces between atoms and molecules like a filter being densely clogged. Once the emotion condenses into a particle, it is more difficult to release from the body. This is where pain, discomfort and eventually disease begin.

So, expressing emotions in their purest energy form is most beneficial. During physical body transformation, the human body moves from a carbon-base cell to a crystalline-base cell to overcome death in the body. It then moves from a diamond-base cell to a bio-plasmid fluid state. This allows the body to move back and forth between matter and energy states.

This is a massive biological morphing process on the planet, allowing the soul to be born or reawakened, if chosen, into all Earth bodies, with unconditional love in the cells; or at the molecular level. This was once a natural DNA function, but was lost due to war, judgment, rage, genetic manipulation, and other destructive excess emotional reactivity and activities from the old Earth and her past universal stories.

How the Quantum Body Processes DNA/RNA Information?
The body is like a (Tesla) magnetic coil sharing an electro-magnetic field with the earth and the cosmic sun. This energy runs through the spinal coil and activates the DNA. When an imaged love focus, of a pure thought, without limits, is imaged for 17 seconds on the frontal lobe, the 7 brain frequencies- hertz, infrared, visible light, X-ray, gamma ray, and cosmic rays- go into action, and they delineate the body's ability to time travel or create other experiences which appear super-human or angelic. This is the greatest secret in all humanity. This knowledge is the lost science of love, which is being rediscovered and will be applied in all systems across the planet to bring changes to: overcome death, disease, and suffering.

The human brain folds space and time via super semi-conductor ionic transmitters. This coil or spiral is so vast that it can connect your brain's membranes to multi-universal membranes, via mini big bangs and black holes through on/off light switches in the brain circuitry. These exist and entry points into/out of matter and anti-matter create black holes and mini big bangs, to both create and resolve universes from the past and future. This is exactly what your brain does when it cycles. This quantum spiral is charged by the magnetic, organic, human heart in a natural state of joy. So, how does your body work in a field of spiraling energy?

The Bio-Electric Magnetic Field makes up the "auras" energy field of light, color, and sound wave frequency patterns, surrounding the body. The field also reflects your general state of balance since, thoughts, feelings, and attitudes that cycle off the: mental, emotional, and physical, energies stored in the body.

The goal, that I will explain as we continue, is to have scalar waves operate at the speed of unconditional love as they pass through the body and its surrounding energy field. Scalar energy is created when two common electromagnetic waves converge from two opposite vectors. When the energy vectors meet, the equal frequencies cancel each other leaving a standing or stationary energy. The space the scalar energy occupies is not a vacuum, but alive with checked and balanced energies. Einstein called them cosmic waves.

Scalar energy is described as having zero frequencies and to be static; a stationary energy that is yet to be evaluated, by our current frequency instruments. This neutral and detached scalar moment, is exactly where love meets life; where experience can be brought in from the universal library of energies to be lived in a your matter container. Your consciousness, the person you are as a soul and spirit, lives inside your own blueprints, relaying through your human personality, which dictates the rest of the story.

However, as these vectors cancel each other out, this scalar energy does not flow as waves, but it does occupy space and increases in spatial mass. When the space it occupies is sufficient, and this varies with persons, the energy expands outward in circles of energy. These circles fold and flow throughout the body's energy fields in a figure eight or spiral. Our universe is the shape of a spiral. The degree of a passionate intended focus in the imagination is a powerful magnetic force for creation in this spiraling field, because it sources continual love through the spiral. This cosmic spiral has 2 counter rotating fields in order to send and receive energies and keeps the soul spirit in balance between positive and negative energies. We could call these the Father/Mother God spirals that nurture all life.

Understanding of Frequencies of Energy:
The bio-energy field is composed of electrical and mechanical energy. This energy comes from the body, and passes through the body as waves of energy measured in frequencies or cycles per second. In its highest frequency spectrum, these electro-magnetic waves are composed of atoms. The neurological system is also electromagnetic; but the source is neurons, not atoms, producing a much lower frequency spectrum. Whereas the nerve's electromagnetism activates muscles, brain, heart and breathing with frequencies from 0 to 25Hz (cycles per second), the human energy field (from atoms) is measured at about 500Hz (cycles per second), or the frequency of light.

All this is to say in the vernacular, that your brain is a quantum love computer. When the neuron circuitry in the brain, the heart, and the pelvic cradle, is lit up like a Christmas tree, and every atom can fuse itself in love; then you are a human angel who has their very own cocoon around their body that has the capacity and velocity of a spacecraft. Now you know what your new Earth body might feel like.

How does my heart center allow me to create change for myself and others?

ARTICLE

Testing Your Power And Beliefs Through Commanding Energies:
Words often hold us to the programming of the lower brain centers. Images and Unconditional feelings allow more freedom to access the higher intuitive brain centers and manifest more rapidly.

Manifesting Change from Unconditional Love:
The less negative programming (right/wrong, anger/joy hate/love, etc.) one has, the quicker you can create for yourself or on behalf of another. The emptying out of life's old baggage leaves a balanced, open, and unconditional space in yourself and your environment, to change or create from, because the heart is not caught in judgment of self or other!

Application:
What thoughts and feelings arise when you command your reality, using these affirming word statements in the 2 lists below? Now replace the statement with one single image or symbol. Compare the results between the words and the use of an impassioned image of what you truly desire. Which gives you more expedient results?

Commanding Energies for Self:

- My responsibility is to be happy and ask for support. I'm here to experience life and learn all I can about myself. This includes my strengths and weaknesses.
- I find out what brings me joy, what my gifts are, and who I wish to share my life.

- Everything that happens to me I create, without exception. I will look in the mirror of others or reflect on myself and ask, 'Why did I choose to create the places, people, and events to happen in my life?'
- I know that I have the power to change anything in my life. This includes self-correction in any moment.
- I'm honest with my feelings. This grounds me and keeps me from spinning into other people's agendas or energy fields.
- I punish or push away those I love when I don't tell the truth about what is really going on with me or how I feel.
- Physical movement helps me master the power in my body and its feelings.
- Honesty tells me if what I'm picking up is my feeling or someone else's feelings.
- I focus on all the good things about myself, not just my negative thoughts and feelings? I master feelings that make me feel like a victim or unworthy, become aware of these, and find ways to fulfill my needs and/or passions so that I feel sure about myself
- I can take charge of my joy and my desires. This reveals my real self. I make friends easily, because people like friends who are open, honest, and true.
- My friends and family take care of their own relationship and feelings. I do not have to act out their feelings or issues for them. Boundaries help me from getting hurt by others. I use the language of compassion with self and others. What I do to another or feel about another, I'm feeling about myself.
- I AM always in the presence of a living, loving God and sustained in a warm satisfying feeling of love.

Commanding Energies for Others:

- What You Give To Self, You give to others as equal god beings:
- I AM the freedom of all people on this planet from any form of tyranny or injustice.
- I AM the healing this day of any one who requires healing.
- I AM the money and I AM the supply this day of any one who requires supply.
- I AM the comfort this day of anyone who requires comfort.
- I AM the revelation of truth and the inspiration of people to seek truth in all that they do.
- I AM divine freedom manifesting in the hearts and minds and in the experience of individuals everywhere.
- I AM the victory and application of cosmic justice to any entity, any commercial endeavor, any government, any activity, any person, any belief system, any religion or ideology that would seek to enslave, that would cause mind control, or the limitation of freedom on the part of any person anywhere.

With the soul spirit activated in my dna, can I change one of my realities at any time?

ARTICLE - *Changing Your Future:*
Man lives in a holographic image of his own God reflection. He lives from the inside of a limited ego- system, or material sense of self, to the Presence of all life with all its multi realities colliding.

Your own hologram is where you're light or experience collides with its own reflection. Inter-dimensional portals create a dimensional warp reality, where the "I" mirrors itself, and opens the illusion of time, showing a full spectrum of light in photon particles, or weave/grid patterns. These portals are the exit and entry points of wormholes or spiral vacuum tunnels into and out of universes or experiences. Because memory is multi-dimensional, whatever thought, feeling, or attitude you've ever had is still recorded in your brain and is still going on now. It can be changed, re-experienced, or deleted from your own brain files at any time. If you decide, to never have another experience of hate, it is removed from all other bodies, dimensions, and time frames you ever existed in, including this one. In other inter-dimensional existences, it was common practice to change from on form to another without losing your original DNA memory map.

This **holographic memory map means**_that the soul spirit, while fully embodied, can travel to any time-space, simply by expressing a loving desire, or using a high frequency tone, because this causes the bending of light. **Love bends light.** Thus, charged passionate thoughts or imagination, **replicates the DNA.** The power of our imagination is capable of expressing and intercepting RNA and DNA from the universal library of information of infinite potentials. So your very thoughts and feelings vibrate to create our reality.

Polarized thoughts: anger, hurt, hatred, travel slower and are denser than loving thoughts, which have a higher consciousness and can manifest more quickly as they travel to the libraries through loving spirals of energy.
When a person wishes to be complete with a thought pattern, like victim-

hood from all the cells in their human body, then those experiences are removed from their personal hologram and are not within their realm. They have moved to a higher frequency, where new thoughts will draw new people, places, circumstances, and events. The movie imaging is then removed from the physical brain via the neo-cortex, leaving room to create a new thought beyond the past. If we feel anger, we can create more of it or, if we love and learn from our anger, then we can vibrate it to the speed of love and can use it for determination or passion, instead!

When we focus, meditate, or enter theta state, we **travel to the void of our origins**, reaching the creation chamber. There are no thoughts or feelings here and the soul can be cleansed and anything changed or created. It is pure, raw, imaginative potential waiting to be expressed through a focusing of energy. The chamber's color is a midnight blue. You could call this the Mother Source/ Matrix energy. If traveling to the Cosmic Sun of Our origins, we could call this the Father Source/ Matrix where what is created from the void of the mother, is directly mirrored in the Father's outer/external light. Their love reflected, integrates both intents.

Future selves allow us to fully play in our imagination, moving in and out of potentials from a spiraling field of quantum energy libraries, to see what we can bring into our now! Futures manifest best in creative play, since that is our natural state. The future opens may possibilities quite naturally if we refuse to recycle our past.

In trying to attain Universal access for information, we re-remember as we return home to higher frequencies our past as: planetary memory, galactic memory, solar memory, and universal memory. Did you notice the ability you have to access any information that you need? Do you remember that your brain is both a sender and receiver and that all your information is already coded in your DNA? Most of us have memories of: deep, hypnotic, systemic programs regarding religion, government, educational, social, and extra-terrestrial programming concerning the major civilizations before, and of Earth. Do you think that you may have come to Earth to heal those memories and evolve beyond them? So, if you met yourself in a future time line, which one would you be? In part two of this book there are exercises to examine such an experience!

Will my transitions from the old to the new earth change my other experiences in the universe?

ARTICLE: - The Science of Love: Confusion into Resolution
Indeed, each density in the entire universe is graduating to its next level, at the end of this 26,000-year solar cycle. Though everyone is a God, there remains the misunderstanding that those beings in the higher dimensions are better or more advanced. They have not chosen the evolutionary Earth path of physical biological ascension; physical material mastery seeded with love in the DNA, as you did. Earth has chosen the loving task as the planet of resolution, for the healing of this universe and every other that has been created.

This has included: the resolution of the violations and distortions of natural and creational universal DNA blueprints; mixed and distorted matrixes from other creations using extreme free will that ended in: time collapses, wars, and a divorce set in illusion between the thoughts, feelings, and emotions of the Mother – Father Creations coded for evolution. Such is the nature of illusion that only matter can create.

The experiment did allow for anyone participating in evolution to attain physical mastery at all densities, rather than simply the non- material planes of existence. The more awakened the cell biology, the more universal access of information and the more multi-physical experience a being is entitled to choose from, without any harm to all of life. This reinstates fail-safe parameters within free will, which were altered in the original DNA.
Even the cross-creational matrixes will either integrate for further growth or return to their own Source. Earth has prepared the movement from a dual biology into multiple flexible DNA helixes or a bio-plasmid system.

<u>This cohesion allows this entire universe</u> and all others, to sort out or realign their blueprint codices, regain lost information, and allow each soul spirit to regain the ability to read their own: DNA blueprints, Divine designs, and resume connections with their soul and spirit families. In other words, there are no beings or parallel aspects in this multi-universe who are not; either feeding you information from the future, a part of your distorted past, or guiding you in this very moment so you can exchange places with a member of one of your soul or spirit families in the next life cycle. It also makes great allowance for your future self to enter lower densities easily and evolve more quickly, due to the diversity and problem solving offered in the experiment.

And do you not feel all the varying realities clashing, one hologram into another, just as the Earth's tectonic plates try to use the ocean waters to soften their movement and expression in order to keep their humans safe as possible, as they awaken into massive change. Whether it is the dropping of a metal pin from your finger, or the shifting of a pinpoint of consciousness in the universe, just the One affects all life everywhere.

Love remains, protecting all experience. Spiritual biological integrity is further restored for those continuing evolutionary studies in the infinite number of alternate Earth perceptions requesting experience. This provides a failsafe re-education for those who wish to understand the responsibility for using energy in matter or those who graduate into using infinite potentials. How would you experience your own multiple holographic emotional expressions in a world of billions of colliding realities? Allow yourself the experience of drawing 13 differing geometric patterns that intersect. There is a "you" in each design, living a different life in a different universe, if you will! If you included a different emphasis on beliefs, feelings, gender, race, and choice of learning; imagine all the experiences existing within you at once?

Every time you fulfill the choices of self-awareness in one of those patterns, is it not possible that you bring that self into the very body you live in now, by collapsing time? Then, all you have ever been, are now, or are going to be in the future exists through the very focus of the thought you are holding now. When that thought is held in an awareness that stems from within, being unconditional or compassionate, the enormity of knowing the self and crossing experiences with the holographic experiences of others opens doors for the expression of love in the physical never before experienced by creation.

Application:

What parallel realities you can create:

Using your imagination, write down 3 other possible parallel lives. Write down what your imagination delivers and let's see what kind of Creator you are!

- Imagine what kinds of beings from other creations you were, prior to this Creation.
- Imagine what kinds of beings you created that got lost from their soul or spirit families and are still looking for help.
- What life forms did you create that live here now?
- Can you design your very own universe using small wooden/plastic pieces or play dough, or something that engages all your organic senses

Is Earth under a divine plan? How does our Earth experiment turn out?

ARTICLE - *A New Paradigm of Soul-Spirit in a Unified Field of Love:* In this universe, the wounded, damaged seeds of four billion years are synthesized in polarity. This includes: genetic lifetime patterns, parental relational patterns, collective unconscious patterns, holographic soul patterns, and the release from soul agreements. Time releases into MULTI-creational time again, and freedom and free will is restored as it becomes based on an inner, emotionally based signaling system. This means that thought, impulse, desire, and instinct direct the focus of love in the way it chooses to be experienced.

Emotions

Love is not a sentiment but a focus from which to create. God can no longer be defined but must be experienced. Emotions are no longer wounded. Pure intention, with creativity based on the intensity and focus of joy, restores the miraculous. Soul technology is the experience of the God-within. We are no longer selling off thoughts, feelings, attitudes, and beliefs for our hearts to get love from an outer experience. We now have free-will choice in the light of other people's choices. Passion and focus cast out any fear naturally, as soul's creational agenda becomes the main focus. Responses do not go to; fear addictions, dysfunctions, control, or false power because a focus that comes from self-love will not allow this. There is a self-correct mechanism in place, which is life, giving onto life. There is an acceptance that all are sharing the same Source energy, differentiated only by an individual focus.

Relationships

Females now carry their inner male inside: Males carry their inner female inside. Self-respect and sacred life replace sacrifice. All family genetics eventually will get blended into one race of peace. We have loved ourselves back into existence, because nothing is taken or given in loving. Relationship is not in bondage, but in service to Spirit. The Soul-Spirit cannot be held hostage, because the heart returns to a pure state of unconditional love: The right to exist is restored.

You will not be able to ignore what you feel. You will not be able to speak about what you haven't experienced. The mind will not be able to rule soul's agenda. The Desire Body has had enough experience that, within a variance of joy, only 2% tension for growth, not 90%, will be allowed.

All emotions exist now, with full experience. Any tension left between love and fear produce a choice for; co-creative joy or self-correction, and altering realities as you go, without being a victim of external circumstances of people, places, time, or events. Group work can now merge into a shared and heightened awareness of shared purpose and cooperation without unhealthy competition.

Relationship is not in bondage, but in service to Spirit. The soul cannot be held hostage, because the heart has returned to its pure state of desire in unconditional experience, harmony, and adventure.

You will not need to mirror others for an emotional signal: You will manifest as your cellular excitement permits, from conscious cells and nerves. All actions are Spirit-cell induced, as no mirrors are needed from the external responses of others.

Decisions are made from a union merge of both inner male and female soul experiences as a unity within the physical body. You will not be able to operate beyond your own truth, because the body has its own signature or signaling system for truth.

The electromagnetic fields are suspended, and a self-induced magnetic Spirit field rules the unified field and quantum body. In short, this means from the God within each being. The quantum body allows desire and joy in freedom because all thoughts, feelings, attitudes, and beliefs are focused on Self-love with an emotional signaling system in the body. With a physical experiential relativistic base, one can now consciously direct and take charge of the joy using past, present, and even future information without harm.

Technically, one can move the body into past, present, or future without interference and in a state of harmlessness.

Respect for Creation

This respect for creation loves everyone back to existence, sanctifies free will, and matter is spiritualized. Your truth is intimate and personal, where the experience enlarges and defines Creator. Your expansion has the potential to allow you to go beyond the Creator as Spiritual Parent. This sets a new model and the next stage for evolution and the creation of material time in physical universes. God-man walks in time and matter while holding 90% to 100% of his Soul-Spirit in the human-hybrid body.

This is a new cosmic prototype of genetic peace without separation from the soul and the Spirit within the human DNA. This heals three levels of separation.

Free will is not just an agreement with many viewpoints, but direct manifestations out of your own flesh, where clairvoyance, clairaudience, and clairsentient beings are natural and normal. Many have called these "light body skills," because they are a higher frequency. A reference point of these skills can be remembered from Atlantis or Lemuria (Mu). Love will evolve from unconditional to eternal, to pure love, to Divine love, to perfect love, to self-realized God love, and on. Initiations are now being taken in the body that was never before possible in the old design. These allow new descending and ascending soul choices and experiences learned from the imposed extreme limitations of dense physical reality and extreme polarity.

The New Paradigm for Future Earth Inhabitants

There is no karmic time or rules, only sovereign beings being directed by the God-within. There are no false archetypes, no healers, no teachers, and no fixing others as the old structures come to a close and are dissolved. The old stories and the old games of enslavement and limitation are left to the libraries. All forms of religion, politics, education, economics, and social structures must have the heart of the mother's bonding inside. The Divine Mother gets to keep her body without destruction. The Divine Father not only makes forms, but also gets to feel the love inside. Yet, this love is interchangeable with the Mother, as one love over and over again.

The adventure is to prototype, not necessarily temples and mystery schools again, but communities that serve the greater good and follow cosmic law, not man's law. The wisdom of the past keeps us in alignment with the new creative impulse of our very own universe. Polarity is synthesized into expansive free will. There is a new genetic blend without the separation from Source in any of the bodies: spiritual, mental, emotional or physical as they operate as one Quantum Body.

It will be impossible to live through another. There is only continual bonding with the Mother/Father principle and sharing an experience with another without losing one's individuality. Synthetic mind is irrelevant and an illusion. The use of Earth's natural rhythms, impulses and cycles replace force and control again. Our bodies are made directly of her materials and subject to that respect and stewardship for her very life.

Expansive play with co-creation and absolute creation for a few, includes an intended, passionate, focus to alter any reality at any time, as any possible wound is checked by experience. The experience monitors the action, within cosmic law, that is checked by direct inspirational triggers from the Divine DNA/RNA, as the will of the Divine carries the passionate focus into action. This makes self-realized, self-intended love also self-correctional, to the impulse of group movements and choices around you. This is a natural protection and regulation from your own energy bands as the body approaches the speed of light and beyond.

Every choice can express with natural bonding of the greater Mother/ Father bond. Any Soul-Spirit gifts are available in the unified field body presenting love from the DNA/RNA firing. So again, a love focus manifests co-creation or direct creation, by taking full charge of the choice of joy and directing it through the unified field with a newly experienced feeling-body triggered from the heart. The love focus maintains a personal soul signature that hears, sees, feels, senses, and speaks directly to Creator. Activity circulates from the personal to the impersonal heart of All That Is as a sourcing and re-sourcing process, bonded to love over and over onto itself.

The ego body is now reintegrated into the lighter frequency-body having given over all its polarized experience to the Spirit. The loving "I" is a privilege and a Divine right. Oneness is the pure thought desire of God felt in the body. God is living you and in gratitude of creation.

Bliss is remembered as a natural state. No re-imprints are possible because soul takes its psychology into an open creative flow into Spirit. Out of this come blended possibilities, choices, and integrative revelations. Love's embodied service to Spirit's expression is in constant inner dialogue. It is a constant union with self, then other, always looking for the next adventure in its own intended and Self-directed expansion.

Thought desires, impulses, instincts, and focuses release from the electromagnetic field into an anti-gravity bandwidth field. The field is generated from these primal feeling triggers in the body that have already overridden collective planetary beliefs, fears, or cellular limitations and appearances. Now, just as a fear would try to reach to the point of wound or excess, time is suspended. All necessary information that is garnered from the already experienced emotion is computed in the brain before any negative alteration for co-creation imaging can occur. The brain imaging outlined in previous chapters allows for each to be the director of their own movie screen or reality.

Simultaneous is the freedom of all the nature kingdoms out of a monotonous state or conditioned matrix behavior. Communication can be resumed with these species; they are also free to access their original genetic functioning, beyond the servitude of humanity. This offers the possibility for some to move from group soul into Soul-Spirit evolution on an individual species basis. This is a dynamic resolution accomplished only through service and the fact that ancient distorted creator beings mixed the four kingdoms with human genetic aberrations in their studies.

PART TWO

Soul Memory Workbook Exercises

The following Soul Memory Workbook exercises are divided into three sections:

4.) **Inner Child Birthing**

5.) **Soul Merge Birthing**

6.) **Spirit Merge Birthing**

These exercises will engage the five senses and open one to a direct connection to the soul spirit.

When performing these exercises, you will feel your deepest conflicts struggle against the play of your dreams and desires. You will find that your imagination quite naturally brings both of these inner worlds into self love, since imaging triggers the DNA/RNA blueprints in the brain, to access information from the soul spirit.

Drawing, journaling, sharing one's feelings, telling one's story, various healing modalities, or kinesthetic activities, all allow for an inner dialogue or soul-spirit speak. This inner contact will trigger the mental, emotional, physical, and spiritual bodies at deeper levels of alignment and self awareness. These four bodies must communicate in unity to remain in harmony. Joyful activities keep us trusting in the presence of life and these four bodies in a unity of expression. We often assign these activities to child's play, because they are natural and normal. Many of us have lost that inner child-like, not "childish", connection.

As you read, you will enter the soul memory storage, which comes in the form of patterns of thoughts, feelings, attitudes, or beliefs. **The ego**

system filters these memories at a comfort level that allows fears and other emotions to be released in a gentle manner. Exercises have been set up to take you through every aspect/cycle of your life to find and release old programs and negative emotions from past baggage. What remains, will be the true self; the one true healer.

Inner Child Birthing Exercises

Memories: The Womb

Before we decide to incarnate onto this planet, we hover over our chosen human mother up to/after one year. There is much negotiation for the best of parents you desire to complete your lesson plans. Yet, at the last minute an agreement can be changed, causing the child to leave, or have difficulties in the womb due, to the discovery of all the harsh negative programming of the parents that must be healed. So, as we enter the womb, we must be prepared to accept our agreements in the DNA and RNA blueprints. We accept that we can complete our lessons or chosen experiences though these biological parents. In this process, ancestral experiences are passed on for resolution, from one generation to another. The goal of the soul is to master positive and negative emotions from past experiences, so they are not recycled in the next existence/life.

Womb Agreements: The emotions we first experience in the womb have a dramatic effect on how we respond to life. Choose from these emotion lists to enjoy the exercises below.

Positive emotions remembered in the womb: Joy, unconditional love, passion, hope, imagination, directed will, impassioned focus, happiness, bliss, ecstasy, choice, acceptance, allowance, desire, dream weaving, faith, inner truth, trust, creative fire, and empowerment.

Negative emotions remembered in the womb:

Anger, rage, judgment, pain, suffering, fear, addiction, thought distortion, hatred, blame, resentment, greed, lust, bondage, obsessions, self indulgence, power delusions, fear of intimacy, competition, confrontations, justification, and war mongering, or any limitation.

Exercise:

Imagine yourself inside your mother's womb at the time of conception.

- What was your mother's egg thinking and feeling when you were conceived?
- What was your father's sperm thinking and feeling at the time of your conception?
- Where they worried about survival?
- Where they experiencing unconditional love?
- What was your response to their fears or joys?
- Where they hoping that you would accomplish what they could not?
- Notice the range of emotions that they pass on to you: Draw a picture of yourself in the womb.
- Were you born naturally, or did you need medical help how has that affected your life now?
- What diseases did you inherent in your DNA/RNA from them?

Exercise:
In Your Private Journal- Record your answers as you image yourself lying in the womb.

1. Do you remember any arguments your parents had, as you image yourself lying in the womb?
2. What special genius/gifts did you bring with you for this life?
3. Notice how your body feels as you write. How does your body process the information? Does it travel from the brain, the heart, or the organs first?
4. Do you remember what your body felt like being in the womb?

Return to the Image of yourself in the womb:
Children will do almost anything for love and acceptance. They are therefore

vulnerable to parental programming, even in the womb, where they sense the thoughts forms and feelings of the parents. These programs get coded into the images in their brain and biological cells within the womb. The child must then live these experiences, accepting or changing these thoughts, feelings, attitudes and beliefs through life's choices. Children born eight years and younger, who have a more evolved DNA, are less susceptible to genetic womb programming from the ancestors/parents.

PROGRAMMING- Polarized Thoughts, Feelings, and Attitudes: can make one feel like they are on a roller coaster: **Use the definitions below,** to assist you in answering these questions with the intent of understanding the polarity programs you inherited from your parents.

Exercise:

- What polarity programs did you accept from your parents? Example = Mothers must suffer **or** be in bliss to care for their children?
- Fathers must work and struggle **or** joyfully manifest all they need to provide for their children?
- What programs most dominate your life?
- Which: feelings, attitudes, or beliefs are you going to change?

The Effect of Negative Thoughts, Feelings, and Attitudes Can Seem to Divide us Against Ourselves:

1. **Feelings:** Long held positive or negative reactions to feelings= **emotions**
    a. I feel unworthy **or** I feel totally confident in myself.

2. **Attitudes:** Long held emotions= **attitudes.**
    a. Being a mother is exhausting and overwhelming **or** being a mom is bliss.

3. **Beliefs:** Long held thoughts= **beliefs**

a. Women are enslaved by their families **or** revered in the role of mother.

- **Mother's thoughts**:
  I'm not sure I can handle 4 children **or** they will help support each other and there will be group joy.

- **Resolved thoughts:**
  My mother was weak **or** my mother did the best she could raising me

- **Father's thoughts:**
  My father told me, you will always fail **or** my dad lived a hard life.

- **Feelings:**
  I must hide my depression **or** I share all my hidden feelings with my wife.

- **Attitudes:**
  I have no time for myself **or** I share fun experiences with my family.

- **Beliefs:**
  Men have to compete to earn a living **or** my work brings me joy and freedom.

Exercise: Again, reconnect with your parents in the womb.

- What dreams did your parents have for you so your DNA would carry a higher evolution than theirs; i.e., what did they want to improve in parenting from the last generation? It only takes three generations to change and upgrade the DNA. Sketch a cartoon story of these dreams. Can it be made into a children's book

- Did your parents picked up their attitudes and beliefs from their parents?

Remembering Grandparents:

Exercise:
The contact you had with your grandparents as a child. Share your memories or create a genetic family tree drawing.

- How did they influence your parents?
- How did they influence you?
- Have you gained insight into your generational patterns?
- What DNA gifts do you find from each side of the family?
- Are there any remaining wounds that you will pass to your children?

Inner Child

Healthy ego development presents at critical growth stages.

It is not till puberty, the most important critical stage that a child's body begins to process the death hormone from the parental generations. The death hormone, or cellular death, is the secretion in the brain and glandular system of addictive DNA, toxic fears, or wounded negative thoughts, feelings, and beliefs that the child must either accept or heal. The child will often carry these for the parents in order to help the parent or gain their acceptance in exchange for love. We all hold many snapshots of negative experiences. Children develop ego mechanisms to protect themselves from hurt, harm, and abandonment. This happens because they cannot defend themselves once wronged by the parent. The child may then shuts down the emotions, leading to depression, anger, stubbornness, competitiveness and rebellion, etc., or disease.

Inner child contact is an opportunity to review any unresolved issues that repeat in your life cycles, relationships, to offer confirmation that it is safe to be loved and love, in a body!

One of the most common experiences, that keep a child locked in memory, is the lack of an explanation as to what has happened to them, after the trauma was over, where no explanation or protection was offered. For the child there is often no one to explain things to them in a way they understand to prevent shock or long term post trauma stress. The child is left to assume that it was their fault that some kind of abuse was perpetrated on them. Early trauma can cause the ego to shatter into addictive life behaviors: reality splits, addictive control, loss/bonding dependencies, or self punishing cycles. So when you go into these memories it is important to let your own inner child know they are safe to express their emotions. In the imaging process, DNA regression, or the theta brain state, you are able to do this.

Exercise:

The process of inner child healing uses all your senses with guided imagery, color, and sound. By simply closing your eyes and focusing on a memory, the potential for healing takes place.

- Close your eyes and focus on the first image that comes up. Do not judge it.

- How old are you? See what you are wearing to get a sense of your age. Where are you? Who is around?

- What is going on in this image? Run it like a movie

- What is the feeling? Feel in your own body what is happening and where you are holding that feeling that hurts. If you cannot sense that, ask the inner child to point to that place on/in the body where the emotions are stuck.

- Can you track the feelings and breathe them out of the body?

- Dialogue with the person or persons in the image, as if they are standing right in front of you, and say what you feel you need to say to resolve, forgive, and create a new outcome.

- List all the senses you engaged to illicit memories.

Healing Through Self Parenting Your Own Inner Child:
Now that you have an understanding of how important your inner child's feelings are, it is time to free him from any **critical parent moment of judgment.**

1. First, close your eyes ask your inner child to describe what he feels. Face the child with your full attention and support and comfort the child in whatever way is needed. Your inner child needs to know that you will meet his needs, or simply listen to his imagination, rather than criticize or judge.

2. Assure the child that you won't let the child ever have to be judged hurt, abandoned, or not heard ever again!

3. The moment will feel complete when the inner child begins to share his true feelings, release a stuck emotion through tears, or explain where you wouldn't listen to his joy.

4. Then identify the area of the body holding the program. Have the child go to that space and ask him what would heal the area. The inner child will guide you by replacing the wound with a natural and joyful image from his own DNA blueprint.

5. If the child is still struggling, image the opposite sex of the same age coming in to assist the child in trusting a friend, so he can again trust you as his adult self. Use this as a playful time.

Connecting with your inner child in an inner meditative focus:

Self Questions with Respect to Different Ages:
Age 3: Picture yourself in your crib/bed. Where is your mother? Where is your father?

- What are you feeling about them?
- Are your needs being met?
- Do you feel loved?

- Have your inner child talk to you about these memories.
- What feelings are you carrying for them in order to be loved?
- Where are your angels? Are you still in contact with them?
- Draw a picture of yourself. Notice the deep feelings that arise. Do you remember moving objects with your thoughts or seeing auras, or your special blend of magic? Do you have that magic now?

Exercise:

- Where you still in communication with your guides and angels?
- Were you able to shut down your natural gifts of knowing intuitively what is going on around you, cutting through the confusion of what people are saying vs. what they really think, etc.?
- Were you afraid to tell your parents that you knew their thoughts or knew what would happen next?
- Did you still talk to the plants and animals?
- Who was your best friend?
- Draw a picture of your favorite toy at that age.
- Did you feel safe to be yourself and trust adults or, did you seal your imagination?
- What is the sentence you remember most from your mother? How did you interpret that?
- What is the sentence you remember most from your father? How did you interpret that?
- What parental conversations did you over hear? Did you like the way your parents related to one another?

<u>**Age 7: This is the age where the child's psychic brain**</u> begins to seal and the gifts are lost, if they are not supported. The child ignores what he/she feels and knows intuitively and begins to accept the parent's collective programming.

Exercise:

<u>**Family Circle**</u>: Put all of your family members in a circle and draw them. Put yourself in the center.

- Talk to each one as if they are standing in front of you. What positive and negative feelings are being reflected back to you with each family member? What are you mirroring for each of them?

- Grandparents: Relax and remember the relationship with your four grandparents. Can you draw them or find an old picture of them?

- Draw a family tree. What **genetic emotional or physical patterns** did you inherit from each side of the family tree? Diabetes, cancer, depression, rage, or victim, would be examples.

- Note the character or gifts from each **ancestral side of the family** as well. Long life, strong body, artistic, scientific skills, or strongly intuitive would be examples.

- Make a list of the patterns that you have already had to face.

<u>**Age 9: This is the game age stage,**</u> where cooperation/competition in performance must be mastered. It is a time when one gets an inner/outer sense of task accomplishment, in order to gauge one's place in the world. This is one's first view of success/failure attitudes.

Exercise:

- What experience do you remember from school that still haunts you?

- What was your mom's attitude toward supporting you in the outside world?

- What was your dad's attitude toward supporting you in the outside world?
- List the strengths and weaknesses your mom gave you.
- List the strengths and weaknesses your dad gave you.
- Did you like who you were at age 9?

Age 12 or 13: Gender role and body self identity are explored at this age. It is where the hormones from past ancestral patterns get activated in the body and the body begins its aging process, until the adult can delete the DNA programming.

Exercise:

- What attitudes about being a man or a woman did you inherit? Do you love your body?
- How do you relate to the opposite gender?
- How do you think the world sees you at this age?
- Will you have a relationship similar to your parents? What changes would you make?

Exercise:

Revisit your Family Circle - Put all of your family members in a circle and draw them. Put yourself in the center. Talk to them from age 12 or 13.

- What positive and negative feelings are being reflected back to you?
- What are you mirroring for each of them?
- Note: list the differences in your reflections in this circle and the one you drew at age 7.

Exercise:

- Draw your circle of friends at age 12 or 13 and put yourself in the middle. What did each friend mirror to you about yourself?
- What was the gift they found in you?
- Were you able to be yourself or did you feel you had to succumb to peer pressure to be accepted?
- How did you handle relationships with the opposite gender during this stage?

Age 17: Make a collage that tells the story of who you were at this age. **This is the age/stage of values and self-identity or first separation from the family**. This can be a highly charged time where the young adult sifts through all the family attitudes to see what fits in to one's emerging life plan and the emerging self. Differing reactions may include: rebellion, fears of divergent thinking, comfortable acceptance, or extreme social pressures. Social matrixes can easily over ride inner genius.

Exercise:

- What values, attitudes and beliefs have you changed since you were 17?
- Are you much different than your parents?
- Make a list of the commonalities/differences you share with your siblings?
- Did your dreams and goals change significantly since age 17?
- Make a paper doll of yourself as if you were going to market yourself for a comic book?
- How did you wish to effect society?

Age 21: This is the stage of acceptance of self as an adult.
Comfort ability comes from having a life plan with a vision of what one has

to offer, as a unique self, in service to that vision. Often it can be associated with either, adjudicating family wounds or carrying on the family genius.

Exercise: Do a self-reflection comparison between age 17 and 21.
Do you feel you have your own sense of self -identity now?
Have you had your first major separation from the family?
Are you family dependant still?
Are you focused on the family wounds or are you expressing the family genius?
What is your present vision for life?

Exploring Significant Relationships
It is sympathetic vibration that magnetically draws us to the people we attract and meet during the course of our lives. Each one plays a very important role in mirroring our wounds or gifts, assisting us on our journey towards a more joyful state of being.

Track Yourself at Intervals of Ten Years: 21, 31, 41, 51, and 61, etc.

- What image did you hold of yourself in relationships, your job, or your goals?
- Are your inner dialogue and your outer voice congruent?
- Plot the major physical, emotional, mental, and inner discoveries. Can you feel the critical changes you made to become who you are now?
- Which areas: career, relationships, health, or finances, were most difficult?
- Is there an emotional pattern that was evident in all of these areas?
- What amazing picture emerges or doesn't of the true self?
- Did you notice your overall attitude at each of these 10 year intervals?

Exercise:

Pick 10 of the Most Important People in Your Life:

Test your intuit quotient with each person to see if you really feel them and their life. Imagine each person standing in front of you and talking to them through your imagination. Look directly in their eyes: ask questions, feel and truly hear their responses.

- What is the wound or the gift they reflect to you? What role are you playing in their life?
- Can you listen and understand their path in compassion and non-judgment, after sharing their life story with you? Did you see their life as they saw it?
- Could you see through the mirrors of their eyes; hear through their ears; and feel how they were touched by life? Did they trust their inner voice and follow their heart?
- Are you able to see their higher purpose without even having an opinion?
- How has your relationship with them changed you or them?
- Look in their eyes again. Now draw a picture of yourself. Have you changed since you started this exercise?

Judgment: Judgment can leave memory imprints that are difficult to change, if you react emotionally to people, places, or events that trigger them. Is there anything or anyone in your life that you have left in judgment, and still do not see the higher purpose of what they are reflecting to you?

Exercise: Draw a picture of this person, such as your boss, or this event such as, being fired. Make a list of all the reactive emotions this person or event stirs in you and answer these questions:

- Are these emotions a part of a pattern of reaction that you experience often?

- Can you allow this person's mirror to reflect something you need to change, show you a new understanding, or see why they were in your life?
- Did you judge yourself when you judged the other person?
- How did this exercise change you?
- How quickly, do you now believe, that you can self correct with a new intention?

Exercise: **Future Self**- Once you clear you're past hurts, it is possible to create anything you want to in your future.

- Be still and bring up an image of your future self.
- Imagine yourself stepping inside a diamond and allow each facet to be a window of choice and opportunity. What window do you choose?
- Allow yourself to see or feel what you create in each alternate reality.
- Allow each facet of the diamond to have a year posted on it. What are you doing in that year?
- Make a list of any resistance or blocks that come up as you view these videos.
- Did you notice the connection with your childhood memories or patterns?
- Now draw one of your future selves.

Negative Emotion Exercise: (Choose emotions from the list following)

- Make a list of the **positive emotions** you most experience in your life.
- Make a list of the **negative emotions** most prevalent in your life.

- What does this tell you about your life? Is there anything you need to change?
- Start with tracking one of your negative emotions: feeling under anger to shame, then under blame to depression, then under forgiveness to neutral or again, love.
- Which emotions could you not get under or were stuck on?
- Did you notice that each feeling has its own story and can be owned and felt as the next emotion arises. Love protects all emotions and actions.

Love Protects All Emotions and Actions:
Exercise:

- If you feel angry, ask what the anger is about?
- When you understand what the emotion is attached to, breath it our of your body and energy field.
- Is there another feeling under that which needs attention? Let each feeling tell its story.
- Notice how feelings have their own progression: sadness, then depression, then hurt, then not feeling loved, then not feeling worthy, till surrender.
- You can also release the old story as you capture the feeling theme in the story.
- Share one of your emotional dramas with another. Can they help you reflect or do they judge?
- What did your drama teach you about yourself? What did you learn about the circumstance, the place, or the event?
- Did your old story change after you told it?
- Are you still holding on to the story or old game?

Positive and Negative Emotions

Positive Emotion

Exercise: (from the lists following)

- Can you tell a story using only positive emotions?
- Did the story tell you what emotions are over reactive and limiting?
- Now pick 5 negative and 5 positive emotions. Use them in one story! Allow your story to help you decide what patterns need more balance in your life.

Negative Emotions

abandonment
afraid
aggressive
anger
annihilating
betrayal
blame
chaotic
cloudy
compulsive
confrontational
control
deceptive
dependency
desperate
disorganized
domineering
doubting
enigmatic
frozen
greed
hate
heavy
hostile
hurt
hurtful
hyperactive
imbalanced
impulsive
inappropriate
inconsistent
intoxicating
isolating
jaded
jealousy
judgment
justification
limited
lost
lust
maladaptive
malicious
manipulation
mistrust
morose
needy
non-functioning
obsessive
pain
passive
pessimistic
powerless
powerlessness
problematic
programmed
psychotic
rage
rage
rejection
rigid
schizoid
self-destructive
self-indulgent
self-prostituting
shame
stress
stuck
stymied
suffering
torture
trauma
tyrant
unclear
unconscious
unenlightened
unimaginative
victim
weak
wounded

Positive Emotions

acceptance
actualizing
adaptable
adaptable
allowance
balance
bliss
caring
changing
clarity
compassion
complete
confident
conscious
cooperative
creative
curious
detachment
determined
discerning
ecstasy
empowered
enduring
engaging
ever-present
excellent
excitement
expansive
expectant
flexible
fluid
free
fulfillment
growing
harmony
hopeful
humorous
imagination
independent
inner-connection
inner-guided
inspiration
inspired
interdependent
inventive
joy
knowing
laughter
light
magnificent
non-reactive
opportunity
organized
passion
perfect
playfulness
pleased
resonant
resourceful
richness
satisfaction
self-assured
self-aware
self-realized
self-reflective
Solution oriented
sovereign
splendid
spontaneous
strong
supportive
survival
tenacious
trusting
unconditional
unified
unlimited
whole

Emotional Dominion:
Children must be allowed to trust the healthy progression of their needs, wants, desires, and joys, through the full circle of their emotional body. Hence, the imagination is based on self worth, self love, and inner directed passion for growth and adventure. The internal biological guidance system is then, not re-active and quite naturally flourishes through finding solutions, rather than using wounding to learn. Imagination is an act of mirroring self in embodied love. **Each time you imagine, you replicate your own God DNA:**

Exercise: Using the positive and negative emotion lists:

- Can you make a weave pattern of **your own DNA**, using many different colors of yarn, or art materials?
- What positive/ negative character traits describe you?

Spiritual depression:
This is often called the dark night of the soul. These major/minor periodic episodes are the result of our trying to keep energy in the lower three seals: ribs, stomach, and back, to avoid releasing negative thoughts, feelings, or attitudes trapped in the body, so the heart can lead.

These **negative and positive cell memory patterns are stored in:**

The lower back = survival and sexuality - effect the kidney /adrenals.

In the stomach = sickness, worthiness and self- identity effect the ovaries/ testes.

In the ribs = power, control and victimization- effecting the liver/spleen.

Examples of Chronic Disease Patterns Complexes:

1) Loss of self worth or self hatred=cancer
2) Sexual guilt=ovarian cysts
3) Chronic loss or grief=diabetes

The life force, creative, or sexual energy must move at the ultra-violet frequency brain cycle of unconditional love through the spine, thus opening the imprints from the immortal gene in the pineal and pituitary glands to keep the body in perfect health. This movement of the life force energy also allows death to be overcome in the body, as well as the prevention of disease. The neuron-chemistry of unconditional love causes cell fusion, whereas, excess negative energy, such as hatred, causes cell fission. The cell fusion is done through the simultaneous communication of the brain, heart, and sacral nerves as they share the same information throughout the body, so that the minute a cell dies, another is regenerated in the body immediately.

Can you surrender, relax and let go of the need to control everything; and trust that our Spirit's energy moving through the body and bringing information will take care of you, with the heart directing love's intent. Our Spirit never allows anything that isn't already coded within our cells to express. This fail safe is naturally built in the DNA in order to resolve a belief or feeling, still remaining on the soul's old blueprints agenda from past stories, so that the energy can be recycled for new creations. We teach ourselves with our negative feelings and beliefs. Can you ask your Spirit for Its strength to pull on the wisdom from these experiences?

Exercise:

- Close your eyes and touch your spine or kidney.
- Close your eyes and touch your belly.
- Close your eyes and touch your ribs.
- Close your eyes and touch your heart.

Write down or share with the group, the patterns, beliefs or themes that come up in your memory in thought or feeling, as you touch/channel your body parts. An example might be; when your diabetes denied long held unworthiness and turned into depression because your mother told you that, "life offers no joy".

New Energy: Can you live without telling your old story over and over and re-imprinting it in your brain? Your limitations will hold on to a guaranteed outcome, to the fear of taking risks, or to the avoidance of an experience that is seems outside your control. Freedom is about total and absolute trust in yourself and the ability to take charge of your joy by being your own authority.

Exercise:

- Close your eyes and sketch yourself four times. Which figure feels the most limiting?
- Which figure feels or has the most freedom?

Soul Spirit Birthing Exercises

Expressing Voices of the Inner Male and Female Soul Selves to Integrate Parallel Lifetimes:

We remember our inner male and female through their gifts and their wounds. This allows us to close out time lines (holograms) that otherwise might never be resolved. One most certainly does not need to repeat an 1859 lifetime of survival, disease, and betrayal over and over in one's cell memory! We choose many lifetimes in order to balance our male and female energies and bring them into harmony in this current time. The soul records each of these experiences, which are stored in the subconscious memory of the body you are no in.

You can access parallel selves in an eyes closed meditative focus or while working with a regression healer in a theta brain wave state. Most often, our parallel aspects are mirrored to us in our daily interaction with other people. The session below demonstrates both access points.

When we consciously connect with them we can: feel these parallel selves sense them, as if they are real, as we observe their experience and the body they are in. How did they feel about themselves, their relationships, their profession, and the society or time line they were drawn into by birth? Each time contact a parallel aspect, you heal or integrate that lifetime within the body you are presently in. The experience serves as a life review and allows for higher vibration energy patterns to be activated and remembered in the DNA, letting go of old, lower vibration patterns.

Session:

A Man's Quest for the Perfect Partner in Divine union:

This client had spent many sessions in theta trance reprogramming lifetimes of abuse he had as a man and as a woman. Many of these were with his divorced wife, old lovers, or even family members from this life. He presented lifetimes as a doctor, a prostitute, jealous lover, scientist, a peasant, rich man of the French royalty, and as an orphan child, a monk, along with many others. He said each session was like watching himself on a video screen. Below, in his journal, he writes an amazing stream of consciousness, or inner dialogue, about the steps for the new partner he was attempting to sculpt and create into his life in Divine union. He said he had been on a quest for his spiritual partner for many years and had never had a satisfying marriage because of it.

His Journal:

Here, he is speaking and writing to **an inner female parallel self**:
"I have learned a new language of Love: I want you to want me as your friend. I accept your passion in this co-ship. I don't want to be ignored, not noticed. I want to be responded to in equality. I want to give this to you too. I want you to receive it from you and share it with you! Please don't push me away, so I can birth my soul! I don't know who you are if I can't feel you. You don't know who I am if you can't feel me!"

"I had many male and female bodies. When I was in a male body I wanted to share all my feelings with my inner female partner. When I was in a female body, I wanted to share all my feelings with my inner male partner. I had many lifetimes where this wasn't possible. I was always looking to reunite my twin selves. I also had lifetimes where I felt this emotionally, mentally, physically, and spiritually in varying degrees, but never solidly all in one body. I have always had to have a relationship with another to accomplish this balance."

On another page he writes: "I often sought to find my inner female self in fantasies with extra marital relationships, or I would have someone love me more than I loved them! I experienced: jealousy, abuse, pain, rejection, abandonment, hurt, rage, and all human emotions I was trying to configure a relationship inside a trapped marriage; just fitting in to cultural, social, political, or gender role. All this seemed at the price of personal love. Impersonal love was something that only seemed to belong to angelic lifetimes, when all I wanted was to experience love in this body! Often my relationship addictions in this life times felt like it was always based on animal feelings, not warm and tender love. I felt dependence and attachment like it was a disorder. It felt like charged passion based on millions of years of an addictive, neuron-chemical morphine drip of: fear, abuse, hurt, abandonment and abject and utter loneliness; the dark night of the soul. I knew it could not be the natural emotions of a free spirit. I was thrown into the dilemma of living in a "maybe state"!

His conclusions were: "Maybe I'm supposed to be my own perfect partner inside first, but how do you do that without a partner for reflection? I have had an increasingly greater relationship with myself with each session. Again, even now, I feel the depth of my emotions arise; the utter, anger and grief and disappointment that is coming from my body's cells. This, not feeling loved, feels overwhelming. I was counting on feeling an equal relationship in passion, respect and creative purpose together! I will make a new agreement with myself. I know if I don't, my cells will die; my body will die, without this love. My grief and anger must not overwhelm my cells. I will move forward into my own truth of my own soul

I don't have to abandon my human male or female self to appease my spirit. I know the other aspects of self at higher frequencies don't have cellular bodies. They need to translate the information from my biology to understand that I'm done with these painful lessons. I want to feel my soul in my body, so my spirit can birth and live inside me. Then I know all of my aspects are healed. I realize that my spirit has become my inner lover and is feeding the relationship deep within me, that I may share it, be nurtured by it, and share it with another"!

In a later contact, the man reported now owning a healing based dating service. His new wife was helping him run it. He said his dreams were now livable, because his inner partner and outer partner both shared in his world.

Exercise:

- Ask to be surrounded by your soul spirit bubble of light.
- Imagine a time line in front of you and follow it backwards.
- What year are you drawn to? Trust the first year that comes to you.

- Are you a man or a woman? You can access this by getting a sense of the clothes.
- What is the emotion you first pick up from this person?
- Notice the quality of his/her character. Ask him/her to tell the story of the wounds then their joys. Can you love this aspect of self back into you and tell them that because of their experience, you are now more evolved than you have ever been.
- Did you remember to trade their wounds for their gifts?

Guidelines for Accessing Prior or Parallel Life Programming:
Repeat the prior exercise, as often as you need to integrate soul aspects. When accessing a parallel or past self, notice what thoughts, feelings, or beliefs you were stuck in or were forced to master, allowing gifts to pass to you from that time. This is simply the resolution and integration of an old self into the person you are now. Most of these will include collective or personal programming. You can journey deeply into their very being to retrieve and resolve old programs.

PROGRAMMING:
Archetypal Patterns: What archetypal patterns did you encounter as your aspects: priestess, warrior, lover, artist, mother, dark master etc?
Emotional, mental, or physical theme patterns: Which of these patterns did you notice? Were they emotional: victim/tyrant, power/powerlessness; mental: "light is better than dark, all governments are oppressive, everyone must go to church"; or Physical: "my body is handicapped, so that makes me unworthy" or "male bodies are better than female bodies". These call for resolution.

Ancestral Memory: What ancestral memory, curses or beliefs stem from the generations before? What was the man/woman carrying in his/her DNA? Examples: "women get to God through a man" or "men are not allowed to express emotions".

Incarnated Aspects: Often we have more than one physical aspect on the planet at a time. One body could be male and another parallel self could be female. Pretend that they meet. Are they learning opposite/similar lessons? How do they relate? Do they feel connected in any way?

Exercise: Allow these steps to help you in the releasing process of your aspects:

- All fear will subside as you: resolve, complete, and integrate the past gently.
- Always dialogue with the soul aspect or human you are releasing.
- Let your aspects know that things are different now, and they have choices if the past can be put to rest, and a new agreement can be accepted.
- Ask them what would bring joy into their life if they could have anything they wanted. Create a symbol, for them so they can re-imprint it in your DNA/brain. Now the past has been changed forever, leaving room for a new potential.
- Stay with them, continuing to dialogue to comfort, if you feel resistance. Continue until the aspect's feelings are complete; otherwise another similar aspect with the same pattern may recycle and need your release.

Healing the Past

Once you have a full understanding of a past/parallel aspect lifetime, it is time to heal it and bring the lessons to the present. All talents, gifts, and abilities are then available in this lifetime. Those chosen lessons need no longer be recycled.

A female Lifetime Pattern:

This story is from a woman who is divorced from an abusive husband and just lost her job from a controlling boss. She was having difficulty attracting the relationship and job she wanted. She was having extreme panic attacks at work when she tried to express herself. Also, she recently discovered a small growth in her throat.

Below is a woman's experience looking at a past lifetime:
"I'm living in the year 1809. I'm experiencing male torture by my present husband. He is controlling me and he punishes me by cutting off my arms so that I'm dependant upon him to eat. He feeds me. My hands are burning. My head feels electricity. My throat can't speak. So rather than surrender, I willed myself to die to get my freedom. I realize my only choices were death or be controlled. I didn't get away when I had the chance! I went so deep inside myself, couldn't reach me. I felt like I was in a black hole, hiding, and withdrawing into my own abandonment."

She asks her goddess-self to speak for her, in order to heal her throat. The angel says, "That's how you controlled him. That's how you punished him. That's how you kept the power. You froze your feelings so he couldn't feel you. You thought that was the only way you could stop his power over you. You shut down your biological and emotional body. You numbed your body sensations and emotions! Then you became no different than him. You were then in the game: of control, of the tyrant, the torture, the enslavement. But death was no real choice? You would only have to incarnate into another life with him to take back your power, creativity, purpose, and your expression. The drain of abandonment by your rage, control by anger has only burned off your true passion"!

The angle continued: 'This same thing happened to you in the soul family! The same thing happened in your marriage and to you, as a child with your family, in this life. No one can abuse you if you express your true and honest feelings. Others need to feel you to know who you are. They need to feel you to know who they are. That is the boundary of love. Those who can't love you will be afraid and walk away".

She then felt her angel breathe violet, pink, and gold light into her whole body. She cried for a long time with grief. After the session she wrote a list of what she had concluded.

Her Conclusions: In a week she had changed her job and left her old relationship. The doctor later reported that the small growth in her throat was gone for, "some unknown reason"!

These are affirmations she wrote about her feelings and beliefs after the Session:

- I will not surrender and give up my self-expression and true feelings to survive.
- Love does not mean the loss of self.
- Love does not mean control, power struggles, that my life force must be stolen! I must not abandon and deny myself to be loved. Love is not enslavement.
- My fear of vulnerability and exposure perpetuates my fears, causing me to shut down my heart and body responses.
- I'm tired of justifying my needs, not feeling safe to love or be loved in the body and holding off my dreams for another or a partner. I will no longer abdicate my joy, my true/real self, or lose my identity.
- I will no longer create by default. I will no longer create only: ½ job, ½ a relationships, or ½ my purpose by holding back.
- No longer will I abdicate myself, limiting what spirit can bring into my life. I will accept and receive what is mine by Divine right!

Accessing Male and Female Emotions

Each one of us carries the energy and emotions of both male and female, regardless of gender body we are in. The female represents home, hearth, children, heart, bonding, unconditional love, relationship, and partnership. She must express her feelings and her creativity. She will feel a vast range of positive and negative emotions and come back to love, knowing that her love protects all emotions. She makes all experiences safe, protecting the right to life and free will. She is the heart of the imagination through the intuitive mind of spirit.

The male supports life in service to the female creations. His nature is manifestation, time, form building, architecture, movement, protection, maintenance, problem solving, boundaries, linear mind, and the preservation of life. His domain is the external reality and its forms, structures, and functions knowing that all actions are sacred.

Session:

Man Client Presents with an Addiction to Extra Marital Affairs:

Inn the early morning hours, the client had a disturbing image that he has come to recognize as either a past lifetime, as these are getting easier to distinguish from dreams for him, or a metaphor for whatever message the body is sending to understand; in an ever so subtle way! There is a sense of struggle and then an image of a man being shot by another woman in a murderous scene. Yes, frightening, but he has learned to set the panic aside and look more closely at the message. He imagined a different scene where the person being shot is now facing him. He has a sense that he was her in another lifetime.

I asked the client first for what was going on and why this other woman was so angry with him in this lifetime. He said the woman caught him with his wife.

This meant that he was essentially betraying or shooting himself.

It was time to look at the motives and beliefs, which drove him to risk creating such an event. The first was that when he was with another person in a relationship outside of his marriage in this lifetime, he was able to feel more like himself; more comfortable sharing and connecting with a stranger. This was sounding familiar. He was beginning to see that this same belief and action was repeated in this other lifetime, as both a man and a woman. The theme was an addiction to betrayal, abandonment, and deception.

The next belief was centered on abandonment. He believed that if, in this lifetime, he poured his heart out to his current wife, he would feel vulnerable. He believed she would see the vulnerability as a weakness and leave the marriage. "Men were supposed to be strong". So in a relationship outside the marriage, he could feel alive, getting a chance to express his passion and experience that feeling of being connected for the brief periods of time he had with another woman. He liked to give to another without the threat of abandonment, as there were no ties anyway in the affair. He felt it was worth the risk just to feel that 'artificial bliss!'

So why is it so difficult for him to express these emotions in his own marriage? Where did the pattern start for him in this lifetime? I asked him to go back to his first sense of abandonment. He described being left at an orphanage and having many families while growing up; never feeling connected and feeling like a "street kid," saying, "They tried, but I never felt their love."

Now, as he has a better understanding of this lifetime, it was time for him to make changes or better choices. First, it was necessary to let him know in this lifetime how important it was for him to resolve this pattern, as it would affect future lifetimes.

His counselor had him go to his wife in this lifetime and ask what he needed from her. He answered," support and non-judgment and for her to understand his passions and needs". He said, "That as he looked into her eyes he felt her depression and sadness of not wanting anything for herself and suddenly he remembered feeling in that past life what she was feeling now."

Conclusion: He decided to take his wife to the ocean. They became absorbed in everything with passion and total enjoyment. He also decided to recommit to his marriage and make new agreements in order to share, rather than control their needs, so they could come into balance without a sense of loss.

The gifts were absorbed while the past was more understood and revelations flowed. Looking at all aspects of this lifetime and others that he has had, there were clearly patterns and beliefs; that relationships are volatile, and where betrayal, abandonment, abuse, anger, violence, force and hurt mix with passion and desires. As a result, he began to shut down the emotions from all the pain and disappointment. Relationships became isolating and the passions and desires along with all the negative emotions sat unexpressed in the body. No wonder his energy level was down before he decided to renew his life.

Exercise - Female Emotions:

- Can you list your unsuccessful behaviors in your current relationships?
- Notice the emotions that come up. What judgments or over-reactions arise?
- Are female: rage, shame, blame, judgment, regret, hatred, and powerlessness different than that of a male?
- How do these feelings affect your intimacy and connection with others?
- Can you intend to set new agreements for equal intimacy by looking at the patterns your partner is mirroring to you?

Exercise - Male Emotions:

- Feel these words and notice your male emotions: structure, money, time, movement, fixing, building, providing. What judgments or reactions arise?
- Check your inner male: are rage, shame, blame, judgment, regret, hatred, and powerlessness different than that of the female? Is the male brain and DNA wired for movement and preservation/ protection?
- Does your male brain feel joy, love, or happiness different from your female brain?
- Make a list of your male and female emotions; have your partner do the same. What do you realize? Notice quality, range, intensity, and addictive responses or habits?

Inner Male and Female Dialogue - the Divine Inner Marriage:

It is important that the male and female energies within your body are in sync. When they are not, it leaves the body in limitation weakness, or disease. If the male emotions are limited, then the right side of the body will be affected. If the female energies are limited, then the left side of the body will be affected.

> ***REMEMBER: There is a direct correlation in healing your inner male/female relationship to all others that you have in the outer world.***

Exercise:
Imagine in your right heart a male aspect of self and in the left heart, a female aspect self.

- Allow the M/F inner selves to communicate, as if they are talking. What do they need from each other? What arguments do they still have? Do they understand and respect each other's feelings? Can they communicate each other's purpose and roles? Do they agree on money, children, tasks, and sexual expression?
- What images of being a woman or a man, or gender role issues, do they still allow to limit their love? Where do they still blame, judge, or abuse the other. Can they move in and out of each other while allowing the other to grow and change? Let each tell their story as you observe their relationship! Was their marriage based on an old agreement?
- How do they plan to resolve and solve these issues? Can they recreate or redesign their marriage? Clarity allows for a new agreement. Allow them to have a ring ceremony when they are ready to recommit to anew agreement and can act as one being.
- Allow the M/F to look inside their video camera in their third eye and actually see their own original mother Divine DNA blueprint located in the pineal gland. Then see the Divine father DNA in the pituitary gland. Now arch them together.
- How does your inner marriage affect your outer marriage or relationship?

Results: How does it feel to free the soul purpose from gender limitations?

- Can you feel the color and weave patterns throughout the body? Now that M/F inner selves have resolved their wounds, can they create again off their original Divine design! Give the brain a symbol to re-initiate that blueprint.
- Now that the M/F have all this experience in form and matter, can they actually read their own DNA potentials, or blueprint using their own imagination. Pretend the blueprint is your book of life. Open the book and read some of your potentials.
- Do you feel there is a direct reflection of your inner male and female to the relationship you are now in?

Soul Family Agreements and Integration:

In the old story of mastering Earth lessons, the positive and negative patterns that we bring to our physical bodies and human families of origin, come from our Soul families. We normally exchange lifetime roles with them. Sometimes they incarnate as our mothers, fathers, children, or vice versa, so that we will learn all the chosen experiences or lessons individually and for the whole group.

Exercise:

- Imagine a circle and ask all the members of your soul family to meet.
- Have each one stand in the middle of the circle and share their expertise.
- Ask if there is something they still would like you to experience for them.
- What polarity lessons do they feel they have left to resolve? Are they done with the story?

- Did anyone in the family have the same experience & perceive it differently?
- Did this reveal anything about family judgments?
- Ask what main agenda or theme or story they want to explore in the human experience once they had resolved their polarity issues such as: teaching, technology, record keeping, or wizardry?
- What new adventure or creation would they like to explore now?
- Grab your soul telephone and call one of your dear members of the soul family that has recently transitioned.
- Have them describe their death experience to you? Then ask them where they are and what they are learning? Or what their new work is?
- Ask them if they are planning to return and take another body? If they have been assigned to be a guide for you, what can they share with the Glory of our Holy Spirit?
- What did you learn about the death process & your ability to communicate beyond the veil?

Soul Gender Bodies:

We choose our bodies so that we can gain the most learning in any given lifetime role and balance any judgments. Often times male soul energies will choose female bodies for the balancing. Often female soul energies will choose male bodies to balance and go beyond gender limitations.

Exercise:

Do you Love your body? Are you stuck on an image of being male or female?

- List all the male emotions you can feel in your body. List all the female emotions you can feel in your body. Is there a balance? Choices for these are listed above under: Accessing Male and Female Emotions.

- Did your body tell you a story about one of these emotions? Did your body resist one of these feelings?
- Did you bring in a color, image, or body sound to balance them?
- Look in the mirror. Do you notice parts of your body that are more male or female? Is there a balance?
- Make a list of your routine. Is there both male and female activity?

Birthing the spirit

When the spirit DNA is reawakened in the body, physic gifts, genius abilities, and a natural joyous/oneness state are natural and normal. Death, disease, and suffering also cease.

The Immortal Gene: Can You Imagine your Body in Radiant Health and 25 Years Old Forever?

1. Go into your perfected DNA blueprint, located in your pineal and pituitary crystalline/diamond glands. Now, re-image your every organ, system, and function, in a perfect regenerative state. You can see envision this as a blue web over your body. Can you breathe the web into your body?

2. If there is any stress or unease in the blue; for example, the liver may be feeling angry or overworked; simply re-imprint it and heal it instantly from the pure DNA blueprint. If a stem cell is needed from one organ to heal/re-imprint another organ, then the master glands make this possible, as well.

Relationship Also Means Being/Feeling One with All Life:

Use the Following Exercises to Enjoy Communing with All Four Kingdoms: Crystals, Plants, Animals, and the Human.

Before beginning, state your communication intent and trust where you are guided. Notice which kingdoms are easiest for you to commune with!

Communing in nature:

Sit on your lawn. What communication comes to you? Do you feel like you could talk to the squirrel, the flower or beetle next to you? What telepathic conversation do you have? When did you last do this as a child?

Communing with Self and Other- Inner voice OR outer voice:

Ask yourself five important questions about your life. Write down 2 answers for each question; the one you think you should do and the one your heart desires. Did you listen to the voice of what social consciousness would have you do, or do you listen to the voice of your inner spirit?

Communing with Soul:

Focus and ask for a vision of a woman/man. Climb into the chosen body. Ask him/her all about their life, meaning their character strengths and weaknesses. Is this an aspect of you? Can you heal the wounds of this person and respect what they were trying to learn? Can you now receive their gifts?

Communing with the Animal, Plant, and Crystal Medicine:

All life has consciousness. Each kingdom offers its power to you to be used for your joy and learning. Notice the animal you meet in the woods. Ask the animal/ plant/crystal for its medicine and how it can serve you.

- Make a list of **3** animals, 3 plants, and 3 crystals.
- Then take a walk in the woods and see if you can telepathically find them.
- Ask them to share their medicine.

Communing with the Elements- Earth, Air, Fire, and Water:

Allow yourself to gaze into a real or imaginary fire until you become the flame. Stare at the cloud till you are floating inside it. Breathe under water with your eyes open. Cover your whole body with mud.

What does your body tell you about these forces of nature? Name a feeling that matches Earth, air, fire, and water.

- What connections do your emotions have with the elements?
- What do your cell molecules have to do with these 4 elements?

Connecting to Your Guides

Spirit Guides, Maters, Angels, Cosmic Beings, Elohim, or Arch Angelic blueprints information/ agreements, are time coded within you. As you learn certain lessons or move on from the experience, you are assigned new guides to complete your next set of: blueprints, energy patterns, or downloaded information from the neurons. These guides represent a certain focus or expertise that you need at any given time. The information you receive from them is processed through neural patterns in the brain, which stimulate the DNA. Because you have free will on this planet, you must ask, or accept this guidance, knowing that you can change/ask for new assistance at any time. The following is a way for you to connect with them to assist you in any area of your life.

If you wish to ensure that the information is in your highest good and the good of all concerned, simply request that no contact is accepted, unless their frequency is from "beyond the light." This protection means that any information must be in alignment with your soul sprit's agenda.

Exercise:

- Ask for an image of a guide to come forth, who is helping you with your next step? What area do you wish to explore: Relationship, career, finances, or life purpose?

- If you are interested in a particular subject area you can ask for someone who is versed in sciences, healing, or the like.

- You can have as many main guides as you allow, or choose to communicate with, for a special purpose/focus.

- Put yourself in your Holy Spirit Bubble of Light and see if you can communicate with several guides at a time? Is the communication in words, images, feelings, impressions, or energy patterns?

- Do you use your: clairaudience, clairvoyance, clairsentience, telepathy, or all of these, when you communicate with them?

Exercise:
<u>Pick a Guide From Each Reality Below to Establish an Inner</u>

Communication:
Using: Questions/answers, light, color, sound or feelings to establish a dialogue. You can also use your: clairaudience, clairvoyance, clairsentience, telepathy, or all of these, when you communicate with them

Choices:

- Your soul (a higher aspect of yourself) or soul families
- A pattern of archetypal energies such as the Divine Mother energies
- A master energy such as the Buddha, Germaine, Christ
- A Diva guide from the plant or crystal kingdoms
- Elementals from earth, air, fire, water, or metal
- Power animals from the Animal kingdom
- A personal guide helping with everyday life
- A teaching Angel or Arch Angel assisting you with your service work

Inner God/Goddess
The inner God/Goddess is your healer within. Below is an exercise to engage them into bringing higher frequencies and information into the physical body. Before you begin, imagine what he/she would look like.

Exercise:
Draw Your Wonderful Vision of Your Journey With God/Goddess.

- Did you have a sense of going upward the spiritual planes, being in the inner Earth, or deep inside your own heart chambers?
- What power animal, spiritual figure or guide did you encounter on your journey inside your body chamber for regeneration?
- Was information received about your next step?

Color, Imagery, and sound

Another way to heal the body is through the use sound/color images. A dissonant color helps to identify the negative thought or emotion that underlies pain and discomfort. Sound releases trauma memory from the cells quickly.

Exercise:

Begin by Closing Your Eyes to See Where in your Body you are Drawn to the Most.

- Describe what you are seeing or feeling: heaviness, tightness, constriction, heat/cold, darkness/lightness, a color, or simply a word will come to you.
- Ask yourself what the sensation of the color represents to you. Is it an old thought or feeling? Can you blow it out with a sound?
- Imagine putting a new feeling or thought to match a color or tone that soothes.
- Continue to breathe with different colors and sounds until you tone the body into balance.
- Pick the color or sound that comes to you when you ask for healing each organ or gland. Did you notice, how quickly, you can create immediate healing within your own system?

Exercise:

- State your intent for healing a particular body part, organ or system.
- Ask God or Goddess to begin at the top of your head and move through the body activating your perfect cell blueprint for every organ, system, and body function for perfect health.
- Feel the movement of energy, see the blueprint, feel the color, as they begin to work. Do this for 7 to 21 days and note your changes.

- Have you noticed the differing healing effects of music, color and light patterns in your daily life?

Creating a New Future

When you begin to understand how you created your past, there will come a point at which you may say, "What's next."? Your life at one time may have been very directed by another's agenda and you were not allowed to experience your own true path. This next section helps you create a future that is very much directed by your own spirit's desires. Allow yourself to fully play in your imagination. Move in and out of potentials to see what you can pull into the present! Let's play!

The exercise below, takes you to the void of your origins. This is the creation chamber. There are no thoughts, feelings and no time. Here the soul can be cleansed and change anything. It is pure, raw, imaginative potential waiting to be expressed through a focusing of energy. The color is a midnight blue. You could call this the Mother Source/ Matrix energy.

Exercise:

When the Soul Family is Ready to Create something New:

Gather your soul family in the creation chamber and bring forth some future potential to be decided on! But first, imagine you're self on a slow descending spiral until you get to a place where you are completely centered and quiet, or see this midnight blue void. Bring forth a symbol for each creation and store it in your heart's treasure chest for when you want to play with it.

- Of the things you brought from the void, did you find your own creations of stars, suns, people, animals, and plants?

- Did you see any weave or energy patterns, DNA codes, holograms, blueprint patterns? Can you draw what you saw? Were your Mother Matrix creation codes there?

- How has the void changed since you last created there? Did you feel wounded the last time there? Did your soul family enjoy being there the last time they created there?

Traveling To the Cosmic Sun of Our Origins-Father Source Matrix

Exercise:
Let's climb inside our bubble of light and allow it to spiral to this awesome Sun.

- Do you have any Creations there? What are they?
- Are your Father Matrix Creation RNA codes there? Describe them.
- Notice how your body reacts in this place.
- Is anyone there to give you a message or exchange information with? What does the sun reflect to you?

Exercise:
Look for your spirit family in the Cosmic Sun and greet them. What is this reunion like? Share this restoration of Divine memory.

- What do you notice about their form, structure, & function? Do you feel an exchange of information?
- How does matter feel here? How does movement feel?
- Are both the Father/Mother Matrix Creation codes there? Havre they changes since you left home?
- Has it changed since you left your Universal Source home?

Experiencing Different Vibration Soul Aspects:
Before we lowered into mass and matter or physical bodies, we created as patterns of light, color, and sound or sacred geometry.

Exercise:

- Travel on a beam of light. Where does it take you? Follow the experience! Repeat this, choosing to visit at least 5 planets in your solar system?

- See if you can find yourself on one of these planets. Notice the body you are in? Are you in your past or the planet's future? What understandings are revealed to you from each planet?

- Imagine yourself as patterns of light weaving in/out of each other's grid pattern. Describe the different geometric patterns you see. Notice the colors and the associated feeling tones with each color. Draw this design as you saw it!

- Feel a chosen color. Travel inside that color and allow it to feed you a new experience. Describe the sensate experience in your body.

- Travel to a planet or system or galaxy that has: mostly ocean life, crystal life, cat life, reptilian life forms, plant forms, elf and fairy life, geometric cities, bird life forms, primordial life forms, a mix of humanoid an ET DNA bodies, or pinpoints of consciousness. What did you bring back from your experience?

- Allow yourself to climb into and then become a: cube, a tetrahedron, Octahedron, icosahedrons, and a dodecahedra. These are 4, 8, 10, and 20-sided geometric figures.

- Each of these four geometric shapes offers an experience on a different plane of reality. What aspect of yourself did you explore in each? Did you notice a difference in the experience according to the number of sides?

- Do these experiences make you appreciate the inter-dimensionality of geometric shapes in your life?

Experiencing Differing Body Vibrations in Your Spiral of Life: Exercise:

1) Sit on the floor in a squared back position.

2) Close your eyes and imagine you are in a lavender bubble of light.

3) Fold your bubble into a spiral. Allow the spiral to travel through

you, inside the Earth and throughout the universe.

4) Tell the story of this body journey. Look through your pineal gland and see/feel the chromosome strands or light strands (telomeres) in your double-helix DNA.

5) While traveling, did you notice any distorted geometric patterns, codes, colors, or sensations that seemed to interfere? If so, how did your body handle it? Did the body feel different, in the spiral, than in the bubble? Did this exercise tell you anything about the capabilities of your body?

6) Allow yourself to hold a real object in your hand. Now imagine it inside your spiral. Using your thought, send it out at the speed of light or beyond. Can you allow the object to change into another form? Can you hold the object and make it disappear? Can you make the object appear in two places at the same time? Can you walk through the wall with the cup without dropping it? Can you suspend the cup in mid air? Allow yourself to move the cup with your thought. Have another hide the cup. Then use your third dimensional sight to find where the cup was placed.

7) Put yourself in your spiral. Now, make yourself disappear. Then, make yourself reappear. Next, walk down the street in your spiral and command the wind to blow or the sun to come out? Telepathically, call your favorite animal to appear and walk with you.

8) Take a glass of water and bless it with an intentional thought to make it taste like honey. Can you charge the water and use it heal an illness?

Systems Programming- Universal, Solar, or Planetary memories:
Most humans have experienced an aspect of themselves in the major time flows such as Lemuria, Atlantis, Egypt, and Peru, and many others. From these times, most of us have deep hypnotic programs around religion, government, educational, social, or extra-terrestrial abuses/hybridizations.

The following exercise will help you to explore deeper into being to fully understand the origin of these programs and beliefs. Whatever talent, gift, or ability we have mastered from another time flow can be accessed from our brain's memory to be used in our present.

Exercise:

- Bring yourself into several of these historical Earth holograms. Ask what the Earth people were seeking to understand about them selves in that civilization. Have they accomplished that or is that still being recycled.
- What didn't you understand about yourself in that civilization that you do now? Did you change that historical time line by visiting it from a newer perception of who you are now?
- Is this the best lifetime you've ever had? Why or why not?
- Can you use the gifts that you had or used in that time line? What are they?

Future selves are parallel selves that are living in the future:

Future selves can be integrated into this memory brain you have now, by changing the past. Once you heal or resolve something or someone you have been in your past; that you, no longer exists in the future. This makes room for more unlimited options to experience and choose from. When you make a choice in the "now", you automatically change the past and the future.

Exercise:

- In an inner focus, pick a past/parallel self. Find a lifetime where a belief from one of your off planet systems is still affecting you in this life. How has connecting with this time changed your future?
- Image that time, dialogue with this aspect, and change any beliefs that are still holding you in wound.
- Forgive and thank this aspect for healing that time in the now and resolving the limitation into freedom.
- Accept the gifts that that aspect mastered in that lifetime or

existence. Don't forget to breathe those old beliefs out of the body. How has connecting with this time changed your future?

Exercise:

- Step into your 12 sided crystal and look out through the sides and remote view the following future dates: 2008, 2012, 2025, 2035, 2050, and 2075.

- For each date view what you are doing, where your family is, and what type of planet you are on. How has Earth changed at each juncture?

- Image, a being from each time. Then ask to be shown a particular skill that you can begin to bring forth in your memory now. This could be: a new technology, a skill such as flying, telepathy with one of the nature kingdoms, or a balanced feeling of joy.

Physical Body Transformation: Healing the Physical Body:

Quantum Physics has proven that emotions condense as energy particles and if they are not expressed, they become lodged in spaces between atoms and molecules like a filter being clogged. Once it becomes a particle, it is more difficult to release from the body. This is where pain, discomfort and eventually disease begin. So, expressing emotions in their purest energy form is most beneficial.

The human body moves from a carbon base to a crystalline cell to overcome death in the body. Then it moves from the diamond cell to a bio-plasmid fluid state. This allows the body to move back and forth between matter and energy states. This is a massive morphing process on the planet to bring the bodies here into unconditional love in the cells. For an in depth understanding refer to: **The Story of Love and Creation.**

Universal Access for Information:

As We Return Home Our Memory Map Takes us in a Sequence.

Planetary memory, galactic memory, solar memory, and universal memory travel us back and forth from our origins, while we are embodied on Earth. Did you notice the ability you have to access any information that you need? Do you remember that your brain is a sender & receiver and that all your information is already coded in your DNA map?

Exercise:

- Allow you body to become a complete crystal, then a diamond, then a fluid bubble. See if you can travel in one of these like a vehicle.
- Draw, write, or explain, your experience of each type of full body feeling.
- Note the differing qualities such as: flexibility, organ changes, movement, emotional flow, blood flow, heart rate, colors, geometric patterns, sound frequencies, gland changes, brain states or changes, nerve & muscle responses, sleep patterns, or any other of a host of possibilities.
- Was there an overall frequency difference in your electro-magnetic field?

Birthing the Soul Spirit in the Body:

Comfort your inner child in your quiet moments by listening to his human needs and allowing him to feel playful and joyful. Assure him that he is a divine angel child of the Mother/father God, with all his soul and spirit aspects living inside his own body with the Source of All That Is.

The Worry Tree: Before your inner child goes to bed, with you, make sure he/she puts all his concerns on his worry tree, so his guardian angel can take away all his troubles while he is asleep!

Exercise:

Bring in Your Composite Universal or 'Christen Angel Self' as a New Guide: Ask these Questions?

1. When will your studies on **Earth School** be completed? Where will you be going next? What: Council so flight, intergalactic organizations,

or Spiritual Orders/offices have you been a member of?

2. Where were you before you came to Earth? When will you have contact with your master over soul group, the inner Earth people, or soul group members?

3. Can you change these agreements?

4. Did you notice the ability you have to access any information you need?

Exercise:

Ask Your Body if IT Feels the Union with Your Holy Spirit:

Spirit, put me on automatic pilot.

Spirit, merge into my body and take me out of time.

Spirit, you bring my focus into the greatest joy you wish to experience now.

Spirit, you meet all my needs in the body now!

Spirit, you make me worthy to stay in my body and have all so need/desire!

Spirit, if I leave my body, make sure you are in it with me so we can return in a few minutes, collapsing time, from our adventure.

Spirit, remove any disruption from my presence now!

Spirit Memories:

Exercise:
Imagine yourself as a planet, a galaxy, a solar system, or a universe.
Let this movie be felt. Could it be, that in some time line you helped creates in these BODIES before earth? What information did you retrieve from your home system? Will you return to revisit your creations?

- Allow yourself to spiral forward and backward in time and see if and how they have changed. Are you changing these places just by visiting them?

- What does this exercise tell you about time? Are past, present, and future all going on at the same time? Can you change the past and the future by changing something in the now moment you are in?

- Every time you image something, can you change the outcome? If you imagine the end of war on the planet, is your world more peaceful and are your human interactions more loving when you return? Can you change the world from your imagination? Is you brain an imaging camera?

Manifesting Change from Love: The less negative polarity programming: right/wrong, anger/joy hate/love, etc.; one has, the quicker they can create for themselves. The wisdom of mastering both sides of an emotion allows a space in the cells to feel choice through a clear balance.

Talking Soul to Soul: Clearing Difficulties with People in your Life: Exercise:

- Imagine yourself in your Holy Spirit lavender Bubble. Then place the person's soul who you are having a disagreement with, in their bubble of light, as if they are right there in front of you. This allows you to dialogue with their higher aspect without having to confront their ego resistances.

- Discuss your anger and their anger in this safe environment. What questions do you have for each other? Listen for the answers or get a sense of how they feel when you speak. Can you forgive each other? If so, a resolution is achieved in the experience. Now room has been made for higher choices, joyful manifestations, and new agreements.

- The result of this interaction during meditation is that the next day at work the boss may became the CEO and you get a raise; or your daughter comes to you and asks how she could take more responsibility around the house; or your friend asks you over for dinner. Pay attention to how the relationship changes.

- What did you learn about love and allowance?
- Pick a feeling or difficult situation you want to change for yourself. Go in your bubble and remove the thoughts or feelings that hold you back and breathe them out of the body! Now replace them with a symbol for what you really would like to create or envision an outcome you would like to create, releasing it in freedom and without conditions, for Spirit to bring it to you. Let the symbol sit in the heart! Does it manifest?
- What did you learn about love and allowance?

Testing Your Power And Beliefs Through Commanding Energies:
Words often hold us to the programming of the lower brain centers. Images, feelings, and symbols allow more freedom to access the higher intuitive brain centers immediately, by passing the neo-cortex in the brain. Use this exercise as a shortcut from: words to feelings to images to symbols for more immediate changes. Your behavior will call for instant self correction.

Exercise:
Pick 10 of these statements and Say them out loud. What thoughts, emotions, or parts of the body do not agree with your words? Notice the changes you desire to make. Exchange the limiting or resisting emotions that the words elicit, with one single positive feeling, image, or symbol. The DNA will record the change instantly.

- My responsibility is to be happy and ask for support. I'm here to experience life and learn all I can about myself. This includes my strengths and weaknesses.
- I discover what brings me joy, what my gifts are, and who I wish to share my life.
- Everything that happens to me I create, without exception. I will look

in the mirror of others or reflect on myself and ask, 'Why did I choose to create the places, people, and events to happen in my life?

- I know that I have the power to change anything in my life. This includes self-correction in any moment.
- I'm honest with my feelings. This grounds me and keeps me from spinning into other people's agendas or energy fields.
- I punish or push away those I love when I don't tell the truth about what is really going on with me.
- Physical movement helps me master the power in my body and its feelings.
- Honesty tells me if what I'm picking up is my feeling or someone else's feelings.
- I focus on all the good things about myself, not just my negative thoughts and feelings?
- I master feelings that make me feel like a victim or unworthy, become aware of these, and find ways to fulfill my needs and/or passions so that I feel sure about myself.
- I can take charge of my joy and my desires. This reveals my real self. I make friends easily, because people like friends who are open, honest, and true.
- My friends and family take care of their own relationship and feelings. I do not have to act out their feelings or issues for them.
- Boundaries or self awareness keeps me from getting hurt by others.
- I use the language of compassion with self and others. What I do to another or feel about another, I'm feeling about myself.
- I Am always in the presence of a living, loving God and sustained in a warm satisfying feeling of love.

- I never make myself wrong. I never go against my god by judging myself.
- I allow the past to leave every cell in my body, through purification in the violet frequency!
- I surround my life, my world, and everything I say and do forever in the invincible protection of the cosmic tube of God light!
- I let no discord enter my being, my world, or anything I say or do.
- I trust, listen, and act, on the voice of my own inner God.
- My past is only a holographic story of my wounds.
- I always ask, "What would love do here?" I Am that Love.
- I AM in my Divine body that overcomes death & aging.
- I AM in a state of love and follow the power and authority of my own Holy Spirit!
- I have never done anything wrong to another and no one can hurt me or take away my God power.
- I have retrieved all lost genetic memory. I forgive all genetic mistakes.
- I can release all deformity, disease, death, and negative thought patterns from every molecule now
- I can release any/all aspects not part of my divine plan and divine blueprint.
- Light is intelligent and does what I ask it to do. I heal myself by breathing in colors that feed me.
- I have given the whole of my past back to Creator and am free to create my future.
- I take back all my power now. I am safe. I am protected. Love protects

me. I replace control with balance and loss for sharing.

- I am beauty, love, mercy, grace, and purity. I AM in the bloom of my purpose.
- I am in total charge of this physical vehicle and can direct each organ, cell, and function.
- The violet frequency color transforms all misunderstandings and all experiences back to love.
- Light is intelligent and does what I ask it to do. I heal myself by breathing in colors that feed me.
- I have given the whole of my past back to Creator and am free to create my future.
- I take back all my power now. I am safe. I am protected. Love protects me.
- No one can live in this body but me. My body is my Holy Temple.
- I am beauty, love, mercy, grace, and purity. I AM in the bloom of my purpose.
- I am in total charge of this physical vehicle and can direct each organ, cell, and function.
- I am master and commander of my world. I am the precipitation, the visible magnetic presence, and the manifestation of whatever I desire.
- I am the heart of God and bring into visible form new and original ideas, accomplishments, and materializations.
- I can release the forces of nature and the power of the elements from limited human consciousness within every atom in my body!

Requesting/decreeing divine grace for others

Whatever we create for ourselves, we can request on behalf of another as well, if in alignment with their spirit. Whatever you command for another, you also receive. This process allows you to make a deposit in another's spiritual bank account till they have a need. It also ensures that the deposit by passes the altered ego which might not be able to receive it due to human programming. Divine Grace, delivered under the soul spirit's intent assures for the highest good of all concerned, with respect for all life plans.

Exercise:
Offer these in Grace. When you say them, use a symbol in a sustained focus to enhance the frequency and speed of reception. Then, answer the questions.

- I AM the freedom of all people on this planet from any form of tyranny or injustice.
- I AM the healing this day of any one who requires healing.
- I AM the money and I AM the supply this day of any one who requires supply.
- I AM the comfort this day of anyone who requires comfort.
- I AM the revelation of truth and the inspiration of people to seek truth in all that they do.
- I AM divine freedom manifesting in the hearts and minds of all humanity.
- I AM the victory and application of cosmic justice to any entity, any commercial endeavor, any government, any activity, any person, any belief system, any religion or ideology that would seek to enslave, that would cause mind control, or the limitation of freedom on the

part of any person anywhere.

1. How does it feel to, give and receive unconditionally, without concern about: interference, investment in outcome, dis-respect for another's life plan, or non-reactive detachment?

2. Are you comfortable commanding energies for others?

3. Did any of the words have a charge on you receiving?

4. Did you notice any judgments, or opinions that interrupted your focus? Could healing be so easy?

Changing Realities:
Human is a Holographic Image of His Own God Spirit Light.

Man peeks out, from a wide gap between his limited programming; his material ego-system, his lower body desires of: survival/sexuality, disease/worth, victim/tyrant, and extreme inclusiveness, into the beautiful Presence or Oneness of all life with great awe! Holograms give meaning to this seemingly incomprehensible paradox, until the revelation that polarities always synthesize back into one love in the human atom cell. Your own hologram is where your precious spirit- light experience collides with its own human reflection .In other words, when you look in the mirror, you meet yourself each time in a possible new reflection of self! Inter-dimensional portals or space time grids can collapse time and warp speed reality, to allow you to chronically peek at yourself in any existence. When you look in the mirror and meet your 'own I" reflection, you see yourself in a full spectrum of: light, photon particles, or weave/grid patterns. These portals are the exit and entry points of wormholes or spiral vacuum tunnels into and out of universes or experiences. This means that all memory and experience is multi-dimensional, and, whatever thought, feeling, or attitude you've ever had is still recorded in your brain and is still going. It can be changed, re-experienced, or deleted from your own brain files at any time.

If you decide to never have another experience of hate, then that experience, is removed from all other bodies, dimensions, and time frames you ever existed in, including this one. This is possible, because the physical body can travel in any time-space that can be remembered in the human brain, while embodied. When following a desire/passion, vibrating sound tones at the frequency of unconditional love, you are essentially bending light. This means that charged, passionate thoughts, or imagination, **replicate the DNA**. The power of our imagination is capable of expressing and intercepting your own RNA and DNA from the universal library of information of quantum potentials. So your very thoughts and feelings vibrate to create your reality, as you select what you want to manifest from the files in the library. Then you can share or internet those files with others on the planet, who want to share your creation.

Polarized thoughts: anger, hurt, hatred, travel slower and are denser, than loving thoughts, which have a higher consciousness and can manifest more quickly! When a person wishes to be through, with thought patterns like victim-hood, then those experiences are removed from their personal hologram and are not within their realm. They have moved to another level where new thoughts will draw new people, places, circumstances, and events.

The movie imaging is then removed from the physical brain via the neo-cortex, leaving room to create a new thought beyond the past. In another example, if we feel anger, we create more of it. If we love and learn from our anger, then we can vibrate it to the speed of loving passion. Now the anger can serve as wisdom.

Exercise

Let's track an experience through your hologram:

1.) Close your eyes. Turn on your brain video and allow yourself to remember the feeling of abandonment or any emotion you choose as a child.

2.) Allow yourself to see it in a lifetime as a man and then, in a lifetime as a woman. Then travel in your imagination and feel this same feeling: in your soul family, on another planet, on another solar system, in your over-soul, in your mother creation, and then, in your father creation. Does your hologram feel like a theme park?

3) Write, draw, or tell a story about each one of these experiences.

   - How did the feeling theme of abandonment, cycle through the hologram?
   - Did it change, strengthen, or add other emotions to it, such as fear or joy?
   - Where you able to change it into something positive such as the search for acceptance? Did you imprint a new outcome on your screen?
   - Did you experience more than one story at a time?
   - Where your images appear flat or did your screen show 3D dimensionality?
   - DID you see objects, people, or energy patterns?
   - What amazing abilities were you able to tap into?

Sacred Geometry

Sacred Geometry uses the five platonic solid patterns as the core blueprints of Creation, for the genesis of all form. This universal science explains the energy patterns that create and unify all life forms in organizational patterns and hold the consciousness of all life for the evolution of the soul spirit. These natural patterns of growth and movement originate in one or more 3D geometric shapes: the tetrahedron, hexahedron, octahedron, dodecahedron, and icosahedrons. These patterns or fractals of creation make up all the molecules of our DNA including the map for the periodic table of our elements. These life codes are visible in: snowflakes, crystal patterns, animal or plant signatures, light patterns, or even spiraling stars, galaxies, and matter universes.

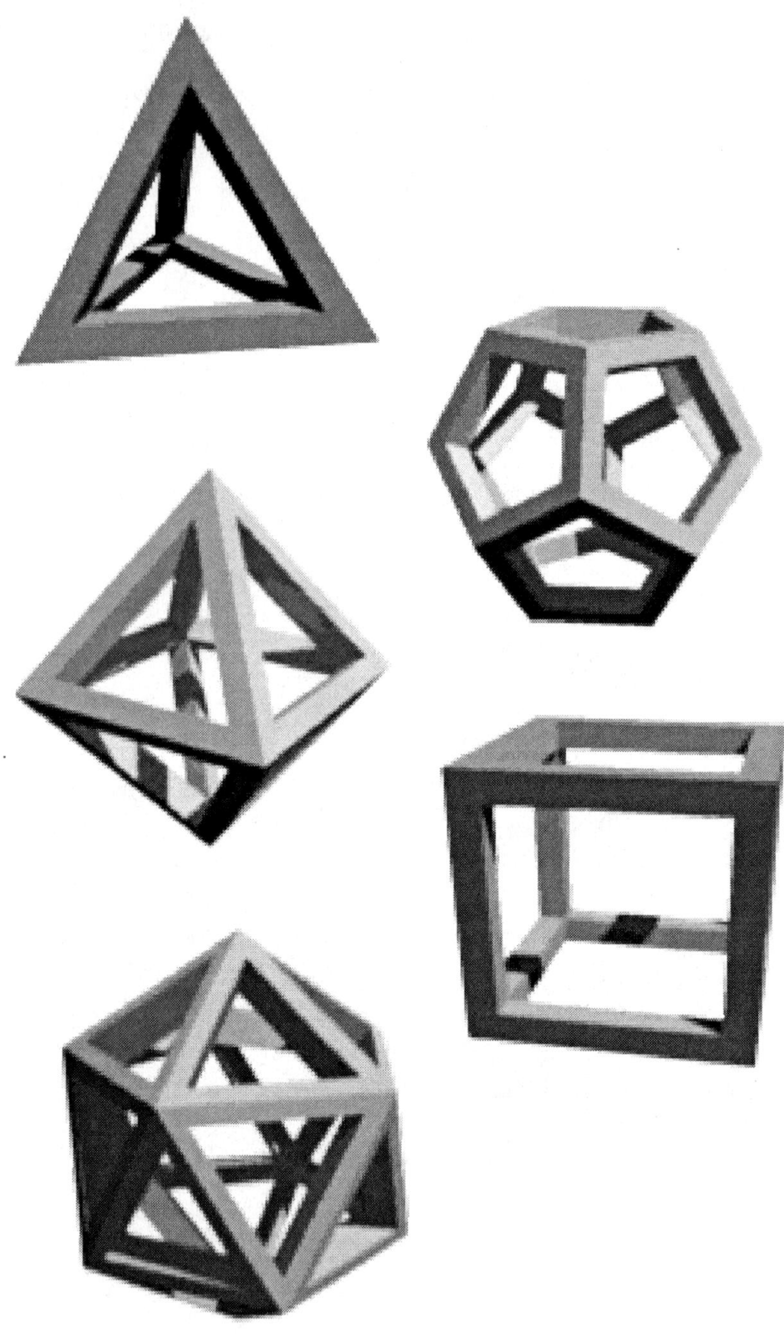

Exercise:

- Draw the basic building blocks of form: square, triangle, rectangle, and circle and insert tiny molecular patterns inside each figure. Does this resemble one of your human cells?
- Close your eyes and imagine how many of these figures might resemble the molecules inside your body in varying **perfect symmetries.**
- Take yourself into a mediation journey and remember when you used sacred geometric blueprints to help create life forms. Did you enjoy creating the human, animal, plant or crystal, weave patterns? Did you use them to create planets or solar systems?
- Can you see how all life is connected? Notice these symmetrical patterns in a leave, on your skin, or in your bone structures?
- Wouldn't it be fun to build one of these 3D forms: the tetrahedron, hexahedron, octahedron, dodecahedron, and icosahedrons?

New Fun Earth Games

These games are designed to enjoy the exploration and trust of altered time space reference perceptions or what we can call altered states of consciousness. On the new Earth, such common play will be natural and joyous.

Light Body Skills and Games Include:

- Clairaudience,
- Clairvoyance,
- Clairsentience,
- Telepathy,
- Telekinetic,
- Bi-location,
- Teleportation,
- Super Physic Skills
- Channeling

Telepath Skills: Each person has a secret they have never told anyone. Guess their dream as they first project their movie to your eye's inner screen. Did you see the movie they projected? Do they want you to share the secret you saw?

Telepath Circle: Have one person in the center of the circle send out a thought and see how many heard it from their mind's clairaudient message.

Ray Game- Color projections: Have one person in the center of the circle send out a clairvoyant message through a color projection and see who can guess it. Try more than one color.

Sensate Intuit Games: Sit toe to toe, or finger to finger, with another in the circle. Merge your energies and try to guess what the other was feeling.

<u>**Stare Trance:**</u> Facing another in the group and eye gazing, can you see another existence or parallel life they are living?

<u>**Flying exercise:**</u> While following another in a fast moving circle with your eyes closed and touching the on ahead of you; go as fast as you can till someone yells "I'm flying", or you all fall down on each other.

<u>**Levitation game:**</u> With a cup/object in the center of the circle; have everyone focus on the object till it starts to rise.

<u>**Time Travel:**</u> **Changing the Future:**

- Have the circle travel into a future calendar year together and change an event/experience.
- When you return share the changes that you feel individually and for the group.

<u>**Body Shape Shift:**</u> With one person in the center of the circle; have each person tell what bodies that person has experienced other than human.

<u>**Body Spinning- Locate Me in the Circle:**</u> Spin one person in the center of the circle clockwise and counter clockwise, with their eyes closed. When they stop, can they find the person they have named in the room?

<u>**Body Trust-Who is doing your massage?**</u> Allow one person in the center of the circle to have any type of back massage. Can their body awareness and feelings guess who gave it to them?

<u>**Trance Dance:**</u>

- Close your eyes and dance alone or with the group to music until you must sit down.
- Do it again with your eyes open.
- Compare and share the differences!

- Did others in the group have similar visions or realizations?

Bubble Body Floor Game: Sit on the floor and roll yourself into a ball with your arms around your knees. Did you bump into anyone? What did your body say?

Who is in the Cocoon: Imagine a cocoon floating in the middle of the circle. Try to guess what life form, the circle partner you're matched with, has hidden inside. Then pretend you let them out and play acts that life form.

Group Teleport: Ask the whole group to agree to focus with their eyes closed and time travel to another historical time: Atlantis, Egypt, or Jupiter.

- When they return, let each person share their adventure. Did anyone have the same experience?
- Can you repeat the exercise and go to a future calendar year? Did anyone end up in the same year?

Gift of Prophesy: Have each person in the group tell about an event that they feel will happen in the next few days, or something wonderful they feel will happen to another, with as many details as possible. Record the Predictions and see how accurate the power of belief or the physic brain can be.

Precipitation Game: In a group focus, have everyone agree to passionately intend to have a delicious hot pizza for 20 minutes without opening the eyes. How did the pizza manifest? (Any group desire can precipitated)

Changelings: Making Objects disappear and Reappear: Agree that the group intention is to stare at a cup or object until it is no longer visible. Now, can you bring it back from where you sent it?

Sculpture Design: See if you can pick 6 people from the group and sculpt them into an object. Let the others guess what they are?

Clair-sound Patterns: Repeat back- drumming, chopsticks, voice, hand patterns given by different people in the group. But, you must do it with your eyes closed and tell who is doing it in the circle as well as repeat back the pattern.

Essences Game:

- Focus on an object, till you are able to change it back to its molecular structure?
- Describe what it looks like to the group or Draw it for them.

Angel Orbs: Using a bottle of soap bubbles from the toy store, see who can blow out their angel bubble and keep it flying the longest? Did your bubble bump into another angel?

Emotional Trust: Earth/Air/Fire/water game- Pick one positive or negative emotion and see who, in the group, can draw an image of it from each of the 4 elements. Ex: anger: volcano could be fire.

Channeling: Hold hands with a partner. Look them in the eyes. Ask each other: for a message, a healing, an image, or a gift from the other's Holy One._

Play dough ET: Imagine you have just visited another planet. Make an image of the beings you saw out of play dough. Did anyone in the group make the same beings?

Slinky Spiral Game:

- Give each member of the group a toy store plastic slinky. Have everyone throw their spiral in the air towards the center of the circle, till they all link at once.
- Did you notice how the link looked like your own DNA strand?
- **DON'T FORGET TO HAVE Fun!**

ISBN 142511012-6

9 781425 110123